IMITATION IN CHILDREN

PAUL GUILLAUME

IMITATION IN CHILDREN

Translated by
ELAINE P. HALPERIN

With a Foreword by
BERNARD KAPLAN

The University of Chicago Press, Chicago and London

International Standard Book Number: 0-226-31045-0
Library of Congress Catalog Card Number: 77-135742
The University of Chicago Press, Chicago 60637
The University of Chicago Press, Ltd., London
© 1971 by The University of Chicago
All rights reserved. Published 1971
Printed in the United States of America

Translated from 2d ed., 1968, *L'Imitation Chez L'Enfant*,
by Paul Guillaume, © 1926, Librairie Félix Alcan,
with the permission of Presses Universitaires
de France

CONTENTS

FOREWORD

Readers of this book who now come upon it for the first time need no one to inform them that in recent years there has been a huge upsurge in the variety and number of translations and reissuances of works which only a relatively short time ago appeared permanently consigned to the limbo of ephemera, shunned by all save burrowing antiquarians, professional historians, or pedants eager to exhibit their scholarly acumen. It does not occasion surprise when such translations and new editions are of works in literature, philosophy, and the humanities — C. P. Snow's other culture — to which the predicate of "progress" is ostensibly inapplicable. But it must surely arouse curiosity when there is translation and republication of empirically oriented works in the putative sciences — those disciplines in which there is supposed to have been a progressive refinement and sophistication of methods of inquiry, coupled with the crescive accumulation of knowledge and elimination of error. For contemporaries involved in such disciplines, the doom of sterility is supposed to afflict those who hesitate to forget the founders, those who become obsessed with the prologue.

Whether or not the orthodox view of scientific activity and scientific change is valid — and there have been serious challenges to this view in recent years from historians of science, philosophers of science, and practitioners in particular sciences — it is still likely that most active inquirers in disciplines claiming scientific respectability will look askance at the reissuance (through translation or not) of hoary relics from a bygone age (that is, more than five or ten years ago). Whatever merit such relics may possess for historians and antiquarians, they will want to know what relevance the work in question has for contemporary issues and controversies within the discipline itself.

Paul Guillaume's *L'imitation chez l'enfant* made its debut more than forty-five years ago in a collection of works devoted to child psychology and pedagogy, edited by Jean Piaget and Ignace Meyerson. Although Guillaume was subsequently to concern himself with general theoretical issues and with the relations between psychology and epistemology, in this work he explicitly disavows any involvement with philosophical issues or controversies. It is therefore incumbent on one who introduces this work to a much later generation of scholars and researchers to highlight, if only sketchily, the pertinence of Guillaume's book to current work in developmental psychology, and specifically in the developmental psychology of imitation. Before doing so, however, one should provide some biographical details about Guillaume's career and also speak about the context in which the present work originated.[1]

Guillaume was born in 1878. Matriculating in philosophy at the Sorbonne near the turn of the century, he was fortunate to be the classmate and friend of Henri Piéron, who was later to become a world-renowned psychophysiologist, the successor to Alfred Binet as editor of *L'Année psychologique* — a Gallic combination, roughly speaking, of the *Psychological Review*, *The Journal of Experimental Psychology*, and the *Psychological Bulletin* — and a living encyclopedia on everything pertaining to psychology. Guillaume's early friendship with Piéron may have had something to do with his subsequent status as a frequent reviewer of foreign and domestic literature for that journal.

After his graduation, Guillaume spent a short period working in a physiological laboratory and then turned to teaching philosophy, first at a lycée in Algeria, then in Paris. During his

1. I am here deeply indebted to necrologies by Piéron and Meyerson.

stay in Paris, he was able to give lecture courses at the Institute of Psychology.

In 1923, he had two experiences which were to influence his life's work decisively. One was his acquaintance with Wolfgang Köhler's seminal volume, *Intelligenzprüfungen an Anthropöiden*, which he was shortly (1927) to translate into French. The other was his meeting with Ignace Meyerson, the scion of an intellectually prominent family, whose father, Emile Meyerson, was a renowned philosopher of science.

The impact of reading Köhler's masterly work extended far beyond inducing Guillaume to translate the book. In later years, Guillaume, in collaboration with Ignace Meyerson, was to undertake a series of important studies on the use of instruments by apes (*Journal de psychologie*, 1930, 1931, 1934, 1937) — a continuation and extension of Köhler's work. Moreover, he was alone to become the principal expositor and exponent of Gestalt theory in France, not only with regard to psychology, but with respect to theory of knowledge and philosophy of science (*La psychologie de la forme*, 1937; *Introduction á la psychologie*, 1942).

The impact of the meeting with Meyerson extended far beyond their long-range collaboration on the above-mentioned research. Indeed, as has already been noted, it was in a collection coedited by Meyerson and Piaget that Guillaume, in 1925, published his doctoral thesis, *L'imitation chez l'enfant*. It was also with Meyerson that Guillaume later assumed the burdens of coediting that other principal French psychological periodical, *Journal de psychologie (normale et pathologique)*.[2]

After a long and fruitful career, Paul Guillaume died on 4 January 1962. Although it would be unwarranted to place him

2. I have omitted from this survey reference to two very important articles pertaining to what is today called "developmental psycholinguistics," both published by Guillaume in *Journal de psychologie, 1927*. These articles, to some extent spinoffs from the section on vocal imitation in the present volume, are discussed in some detail in Arthur Blumenthal's book *Language and Psychology: Historical Aspects of Psycholinguistics* (New York: John Wiley, in press)

in the top rank of twentieth-century French-writing psychologists — with such men as Piéron, Piaget, and Wallon — his con-
tributions as an author, a translator, and an editor are generally
acknowledged to have been of high quality and to have done
much to provide a certain tone to the French psychological
scene during the second quarter of the century.

Now a few words about the context in which the present
work was embedded when it was originally issued. Whatever
elements a work possesses that allow it to transcend its specific
place, time, and circumstances — and here only the future can
determine what survives of the past — there is no doubt that
the style and substance of many arguments in a work can be
understood only in terms of a climate of opinion and a universe of discourse which may have subsequently disintegrated.
Where there has been a dissolution of the universe of discourse
in which the work was conceived, many of the explicit theses
and arguments of the work, which have presupposed that universe, may seem to lose their clarity, cogency, and even comprehensibility. On the other hand, if the older climate of opinion and universe of discourse are not dissolved but are merely
dormant, then the reawakening may well restore the cogency
and comprehensibility — in a word, the *relevance* — of a work
that appeared for a while to be devoid of any current interest.

As the reader may easily discern by a quick glance at the list
of references in the back of this book, Guillaume's "reference
group" comprised a composite of "grand theory" developmen-
talists (e.g., Herbert Spencer, James Mark Baldwin, L. T. Hobhouse), precursors of modern ethology (Craig, Conradi), pio-
neers in the naturalistic study of infant behavior (e.g., Preyer,
Compayre, Sully), close students of the emergence and formation of language in the child (e.g., the Sterns, the Scupins, Pavlo-
vitch, O. Bloch, and Piaget), Gestaltists such as Köhler and
Koffka, and early behaviorists (Thorndike, Watson).

Although some concerns of the scholars belonging to this reference group were, for a period, in suspended animation, and
although some of their terminological innovations have been

superseded, it should be reasonably clear that the period in which Guillaume's book first appeared was one in which anti-instinctivists were challenging those who seemed ritually to invoke instinct and preformation; exponents of structure and system were at odds with the atomists and elementarists; mechanists and behaviorists had locked horns with proponents of teleology and mentalism; and those opting for discontinuities of form and function in phylogenesis and ontogenesis were controverted by those who insisted on continuity. In sum, it was a period very much like the present. And because Paul Guillaume, in this work, attempts with regard to imitation in the child to grapple with all of these fundamental issues and controversies, his book has today regained the relevance that it had nearly half a century ago.

There is one further point to be made with regard to the prevailing climate of opinion about developmental psychology in the 1920s — and perhaps in the 1970s: that point has to do with method of inquiry. Often regarded as the method of choice, or at least as a widely accepted and widely practiced method, long-range (longitudinal), sympathetic, naturalistic observation coupled with ad hoc "little quasi-experiments" — typically on one's own children or else on relatives — was used by investigators as the basis for drawing general and ostensibly universal conclusions concerning "the development of language in the child," "the development of thought in the child," and so on. Unencumbered by methodological or methodolatrous interdictions about the need for representative sampling, experimental controls, observer bias, etc., students of child development proceeded on the assumption that "if you've seen one child (or perhaps two) you've seen them all." Of course, there would doubtless be individual variations in rate or tempo, but it was tacitly assumed that the structure, sequence, and causal relations involved in developmental change were universal and could be observed in any specimen of *Homo sapiens*.[3]

---

3. Where seemingly different patterns of development were reported by other students of child life using the same method, these would, as in psy-

Although with slight reservations, Guillaume adopted this method of inquiry: "Writers agree that in order to be fruitful, psychological observation should be confined to subjects whose mental evolution can be closely followed. I have tried to comply with this conclusion by studying my own children during the first two years of life" (p. 1).

As one knows, this method was subsequently subjected, and continues to be subjected, to severe criticism, despite the fact that variants of it have been employed by those psychologists widely taken as having the most seminal influence on the discipline (e.g., Freud, Piaget). This is not the place to deal with the *Methodenstreit* of contemporary psychology. One may remark, however, that the method used by Guillaume and others has recently seemed to gain favor among many psychologists previously addicted to experimental methodology with large samples; for example, in the domain of developmetal psycholinguistics.

Let us turn finally to the relevance of Guillaume's book to the contemporary scene in developmental psychology, particularly to the developmental psychology of imitation. From the point of view of the current reader and research worker, *Imitation in Children* is pertinent for at least three reasons.

One reason has to do with the relative *stasis of inquiry* in the area of concern to Guillaume. In a recent examination of "the problem of imitation" (1969), Justin Aronfreed [4] introduces his discussion by citing a statement made by a British psychologist (C. W. Valentine) who wrote only shortly after the publication of Guillaume's book. The statement was to the effect that psychology of imitation is in a chaotic state, owing partly to the uncertain and equivocal reference of the term and deriving, in part, from a disagreement as to the facts. Aronfreed comments that this assessment is equally applicable today, despite the

choanalysis, be employed as the basis for revising and reformulating "universals in development."

4. In L. Lipsitt and H. W. Reese, eds., *Advances in Child Development and Behavior*, vol. 4. New York: Academic Press.

emergence of a number of new approaches to the definition and study of imitation. Given this state of affairs, any sustained work on the development of imitation is, in a sense, a contemporary work and has something to contribute to a future synthesis.

A second reason stems paradoxically from the popularity of Piaget. In *Play, Dreams and Imitation*, Piaget often cites Guillaume's treatise. Although Guillaume clearly wrote from an orientation different from that of Piaget, the character and degree of refinement of his observations and analyses are comparable, and hence merit the attention and scrutiny of those who find Piaget's work fascinating.

Finally, Guillaume's book in itself is one of the few major attempts by a perceptive mind to deal with the *processes* involved in the final achievement of "true imitation." Unlike many psychologists whose primary concerns are with the effects of imitation or the functions of imitation, Guillaume devotes his entire work to a critical analysis of the "mechanisms" by which the instinctive or reflexive movements of the newborn are transformed into imitations of the movements of others.

It is unnecessary to list here the main theses of this work. The reader can determine them for himself.

BERNARD KAPLAN
Clark University

INTRODUCTION

Many people have studied the phenomenon of imitation: psychologists, physicians, naturalists, and sociologists have all shown an interest in it. Theories like those of Tarde and Baldwin amount to philosophies of imitation. But the effects of imitation and the role it plays in social life have been examined far more thoroughly than its psychological mechanism. In general, there is a moment in the development of every individual at which the origins of this perfectly established mechanism cease to be perceptible. It would be helpful to apprehend this phenomenon from its inception in the very young child. Writers agree that in order to be fruitful, psychological observation should be confined to subjects whose mental evolution can be closely followed. I have tried to comply with this conclusion by studying my own children during the first two years of life.

Such an undertaking cannot limit itself to recording observations. Psychological literature abounds in unquestionably valuable monographs on children, but few general conclusions have been drawn from them. The various theories must therefore be considered and discussed on the basis of data contributed by others as well as by myself. Such a study will enable me to indicate difficulties that have been overlooked and perhaps to state the problem more clearly. The importance attributed to minute and very banal data — however especially appealing they might be for the author — may be attributed solely to preoccupation with methodology.

Imitation conforms to general psychophysiological laws governing the production of movement. I will therefore begin by reviewing the findings of works on contemporary psychology that deal with this essential question.

The second part of this study will be devoted to a relatively simple phenomenon, vocal imitation, which happens to be the subject of the best study produced so far. It will serve as a guide in the third part of this book where I take up the more general and complex problem of observable imitation of acts.

In the fourth section I will examine the relation of imitation to the beginnings of personal awareness; in the fifth, my attention will be focused on the affective aspects of imitation.

Finally, the results obtained through observation of the child will be compared with data on similar problems already available in studies of animal psychology.

Observations about a child are significant only if the age of the subject is recorded. I have adopted the following system: the first number given designates the month, the second, the day. This chronology has importance only for the individual. As in physical growth, the order in which data appear is more important than absolute age. The children are identified by their initials: P for Paul and L for Louise. The reader may find it helpful to know that throughout the period when Paul was under observation, he spent very little time with other children, whereas Louise, our younger child, had the company of her brother who is six years her senior. Their physical and mental development was normal.

PSYCHOLOGICAL
ASPECTS OF
MOVEMENT

I

Instinct and Habit. Every movement results from a stimulus transmitted to the muscles either directly or through the nervous system. The term spontaneous or impulsive movement probably conceals our ignorance of the true origins of internal or external, conscious or unconscious, stimuli.

Stimuli that stem from the nervous system can have either a general or a particular effect. The former involves the phenomenon of diffuse dynamogenesis (an increase in activity caused by sensory stimulation) or inhibition. Psychologists today are familiar with the motor properties of perceptions, emotions, and ideas. But the stimulus, owing to its specific nature as well as to the preformed structure of the nervous system, often produces even more specific responses, which may be called reflexes, if one takes the word in the general sense in which physiologists use it and not in the narrower sense employed by the medical vocabulary. In this sense, there is no need to distinguish between instinct and reflex. These terms will be used to cover all innate reactions to a stimulus of internal or external origin. Such an a priori definition doubtless implies an arbitrary solution to an important philosophical problem. But there is no space to discuss this in a study as specialized as ours, and we must choose a working hypothesis.

Hereditary determinism is different from the determinism of individual *habits*, of acquired ways of reacting to certain stimuli. The law that governs these habits is perhaps the soundest part of all our psychological knowledge. It pertains to the *transference* of motor power which moves from efficient stimuli to initially inefficient ones, the latter coming first in a certain number of experiments.

This law was first illustrated in the studies of physiologists (Pavlov, Bechterev) on the conditioned reflex. A bitter substance placed on the tongue of an animal causes salivary secretion; an electric shock applied to the extremity of a limb determines its flexion (hereditary, unconditional reflexes). On the other hand, any stimulus (sound, light, contact) that regularly preceded the first one would itself ultimately produce salivary secretion or the flexing of a limb. This principle is identical with the law of *recurrence* that Hachet-Souplet applies to training. By introducing a certain signal (gesture or word) before the action of an instinctive stimulant, one communicates its force. This signal will in turn become necessary when, because of the same law, each phase of the act, taught separately at first, will be set in motion by the sensations that the execution of the preceding act engenders.

An analogous mechanism occurs in habits that animals contract without any artificial training. The one difference is that definitive associations are established only after trial and error. We will return to this later. Here we must recall the experiments conducted by the American school. These showed that animals can by themselves learn to get out of cages (by maneuvering mechanisms), recognize the boxes in which their food has been hidden, run mazes, etc. Above all, we must demonstrate how, in nature, they manage to regulate their acts according to cues that make possible motor anticipation; how their activity becomes subordinate to the rhythm of external phenomena; how such things as mating or inhibition are carried out; and how the animals are able to produce the special instincts that respond to particular environmental conditions (habitat, relations with others, etc.). In all these instances we encounter examples of the law of transference.

The same applies to human habits. An analysis of any acquired activity will make this plain. A pianist who reads music learns to subordinate the movements of his fingers to

certain visual cues (notes read from a score), which are thus
substituted for any prior motor images. When he learns a piece
by heart, each note heard or each movement of the fingers felt
becomes a signal for the execution of the following note, thus
sparing him the need to read the music. Such transferences are
entirely parallel to those mentioned earlier in regard to training.

It would be surprising if this general principle were not
abundantly represented in a study of children. On every page
of this book there will be occasion to apply it. The entire development of the child from early infancy onward consists of reactions to increasingly early signals about happenings that
interest him. His intellectual growth takes place through the
transference of an acquired affective and motor property to a
great many perceptions that become significant and usable.

Although the principle is well established today, it is nonetheless necessary to clarify the meaning of certain terms of any
given statement.

In what sense does perception determine movement? Apart
from the metaphysical and methodological problems that this
question may raise, we ask whether, as the epiphenomenist doctrine claims, physiological excitation alone plays such a role.
Should an efficiency of its own be attributed to the subjective
modification that accompanies it, as certain spiritualist doc-
trines hold? This problem has no experimental significance
because one cannot separate *in man* the two aspects, objective
and subjective, and attribute to one of them a particular causality. On the other hand, since awareness can be ascertained only
by the subject who is observing himself, it is legitimate and
prudent in animal psychology to speak only in objective terms.
When applied to *the child*, however, the statement: "Perception determines movement" is, I believe, devoid of serious
ambiguity.

It is more important to be precise about the meaning of the
word *determinism*. Quinine placed on the tongue stimulates
salivary secretion. The use of quinine is almost always sufficient,
and the result is almost invariable. Similarly, the lash of a whip

produces a movement of retreat; a burn leads to a sudden with-
drawal of the injured member, etc. The same is not altogether
true of other causes one might substitute for these. The result
is more variable; secondary circumstances play a certain role.
More pronouncedly, the sight of musical notes written on a
score does not determine the movements of the musician, in the
strict sense of the word. Apart from unconditioned reflexes,
there is an entire category of reactions, notably emotional, that
may to a certain extent be arrested or modified by a deliberate
effort. There are other reactions, however, in which no effort at
all seems necessary to modify their automatic nature. At the
most we note a certain strain if will power should intervene only
after such automatism is already under way.

It would be better, therefore, to say in this connection that
perception *regulates* or governs the reaction. Determinism in
this case is a complex phenomenon. In the instance of simple
reaction to pain, sensation is intensely affective; it dictates the reaction even as it determines the form, depending upon the
nature and location of the pain. In the complex acts considered
here, there is a disparity between the purely affective factors
(desire, aversion, or willful execution of an act) and the necessary but not sufficient intellectual ones. One does not act, one
does not imitate, either because one does not *wish* to, or because one does not *know how* to behave or imitate. The term
regulation therefore indicates only partial determinism. The
perception-signals are merely *factors* in the action. To provide
a complete explanation, the entire mental state must be taken
into account. Yet we can foresee that in any somewhat simplified
psychic state (absent-mindedness, fatigue) these causes will
again become fully determinate through the suppression of inhibiting influences exerted by a more complex state of mind.

The Meaning of the Law of Transference. We prefer the term
law of transference (often used by Ribot) to the more classical
formulation, law of association. One might see in this an example of the association of ideas. A perception (the sight of the

whip) may awaken a memory (the pain of the blow) and this memory will develop affective motor consequences of its own (fear, flight). Perception will thus operate only through the revival of a past state of consciousness. But will such an interpretation always be valid? Internal observation, whose evidence cannot be considered decisive here, tends to lead us to doubt the regular existence of this intermediary. Not only does repetition tend to obscure it, if it is present, so that the evocation of justificatory memories becomes impossible, but one cannot even be sure of its continuous existence throughout the first habit-forming stage. It might be that memory, developed in autonomous images, constitutes a form of superior thought that is perhaps uniquely human, and even exceptional in man, whereas the formation of habits through the transference of motor properties to associated stimuli seems to be a much more general fact.

Moreover, in speaking of an association of stimuli we are merely expressing the external conditions related to the formation of habits; we shall not permit ourselves to hypothesize about what is happening in the nerve centers. If excitation, at first inefficient, becomes motor, is the change due to cerebral interference with efficient primitive *sensory* excitation? Or does it occur merely because excitation becomes involved in the pathways opened by the *motor* innervation with which it coincides in time? Should we say with Thorndike that the essential fact about habit formation is not the association of two perceptions but the association of one perception with a motor impulse (set in motion, to be sure, by the other perception)? If this were so, the awakening of a "justificatory" memory of the primitive stimulant would constitute a possible complication in the transference, but not the initial or general prerequisite of the process.

However, the concept as we have stated it here is also distinctive because of a characteristic unrelated to the association of ideas, at least as the latter is generally understood. The order of the succession of facts is neither unaffected nor reversible.

The excitation which precedes assumes the reactions of the stimulus that follows, but the reverse is not true. From a strictly associative point of view, there is already reason to entertain some reservations about this presumed indifference of the meaning of associations. To learn is to connect memories in a certain order. When reciting a lesson, this can be altered only by a difficult though secondary operation. To know how to translate a text from one language to another does not imply that one can do the reverse; someone who knows how to translate may be incapable of composing. The reversibility of the association of a word with a thing is nothing less than direct: to speak a language, even one's native tongue, differs quite distinctly from understanding it. More generally, in any current of thought there is a direction, a natural inclination, which is difficult to trace. But in a study of the transference of motor impulses there is not the slightest justification for accepting the notion of such a reversibility. To imagine what it was in a past experience that preceded an occurrence similar to the event we are witnessing today is an intellectual assumption that leads to a practical approach only by a detour. It is about the consequence, not the antecedent of an occurrence, that one needs to know directly through analogy, since one must adapt oneself to the immediate future rather than to the past. The normal function of transference is to set the stage for reactions; one's thoughts return to the past only to meet the future with greater assurance.

II

The Mental Image and Habitual Automatism. At this point there arises a difficulty that we must examine in depth when dealing with the psychology of imitation.

An implicit or explicit thesis to be found in many books on psychology pictures the mental image of an act as "an act that begins" (Ribot). The effect described becomes a motivating cause. This would be true not only of a deliberate act, in the narrow sense of the word, but also of the various forms of psychological automatism. The impulsive force of a fixed idea or of suggestion is that of an image of the act or of its consequences. This theory is applied to the very initiation of the act. If, when the act has become habitual, it suffices to imagine its effects, then one should have visualized from the very start the means of executing it — in other words, the movements themselves. This image is but the memory of the sensations that accompanied their accidental execution. Thus the perception of movement, that is, its effect on consciousness, will become, through the memory of it, a condition for reproducing this same movement.

This concept is based on facts. Nonetheless, it apparently contradicts the theory of recurrence. Can perception of an accomplished act constitute a condition for its subsequent execution? According to the law of recurrence, it can only lead to the immediate execution of another movement for which it had become the signal. But then how can the memory image of a movement possess motor properties which the corresponding perception does not possess?

In fact, in all constituted habits, perception of the first phase of the act determines the execution of the act that follows. When I go up the stairs, the sensations caused by the position of one foot do not tend to make me recommence an accomplished movement but rather to regulate the movement of the other foot (Woodworth). Expressed in more general terms, all our habitual acts constitute a long chain of movements, each of which provides, consciously or not, a stimulus for the movement that follows. Diseases that disorganize the perception of movements as they occur are diagnosed as ataxias. What is missing is not the original impulse but the automatic regulation whereby what remains to be accomplished is made to hinge at every moment on what has just been accomplished. Consequently, the coordination of partial movements, the arrest, moderation, or correction within the desired time of an initial gesture, are defective. For the same reason, the original impulse itself is more or less eliminated when all perception of the *initial position* of an arm or leg disappears. Each phase therefore depends on stimuli engendered by the *preceding* phase.

If we observe ourselves in our daily lives, we find that *before* performing an act we rarely imagine ourselves in the process of performing it; nor do we even imagine what we are about to do. But we perceive the signals that determine the act, the clues that limit it in space, and the objects and people to which it is addressed. The soldier who fires a gun on command (ready, fire!) is obeying external signals. But for the practiced hunter who fires spontaneously, the act conforms no less closely to complex perceptions of weapon, wild game, and obstacles, without the usual interposition of a striking image that anticipates the fact. Perceptions not only govern an act, they suggest it. I do not mean by this that they suggest the *idea*, the image. Rather, they directly determine the execution of an act without the intermediary of a mental picture of the act itself.

Even an attempt to visualize such an image will not always be successful. As has often been said, muscular contractions are not visualized because consciousness is unaware of muscles. We will not know what muscles are involved in phonation, articulation, movements of the head and fingers, etc., until we have made a special study of anatomy. But we must go even further. We have no general knowledge about the *tangible and visible elements* of movements themselves. If, before I have executed it, I try to imagine the act of climbing the stairs or of putting my foot on the rung of a chair upon which I am seated, I will notice when I do it that I have nowise anticipated the first phases of the act (the backward movement of the body toward the opposite direction of that of the leg that is moving, etc.). The mind's image therefore corresponds imperfectly to that which we observe after the fact. This would apply even to far more complicated examples.

In most cases, an image of the movement to be executed is so unnecessary that its interposition can be disturbing. One observes this in those habitual gestures, speech, writing, etc., to which one would like to give particular care. Such parasitical images disorganize the normal play of sensory-motor reactions.

Nevertheless, there is no doubt that one often pictures an act before executing it. But we must eliminate instances in which the image does not relate to the execution of an act but rather to our conception of it or deliberation about it. In this kind of preparatory phase, the image is necessary. Perception of the external world is virtually a permanent appeal to an enormous number of well-defined instinctive or habitual activities. But these activities remain latent and become real only under the impact of images that clarify the necessity or opportunity to act, or that do away with the inhibitions that hampered them. It is mainly when such a problem arises that an image appears in one's consciousness. We visualize the act because we want to evaluate it or find out how others will judge it. We perform the act in our minds in order to produce affective reactions and judge them. Basically, the same thing is true when the image relates to the choice of means for the accomplishment of an already well-defined end. Ideally, various means are first tried, and from these one makes a selection; but all this happens in our minds. We also visualize something we very much desire — not merely the object but sometimes also the act itself. But the conflict between the unfolding of the action and the appearance of the image has often been pointed out. Thinking about the act appears to be a substitute for an impossible or inopportune action. We dream of action when we do not act and, one might say, to the extent that we do not act.

III

The Mental Image and New Adaptations. But the foregoing discussion does not contain all the answers to the question.

If, until now, we have not perceived the role of the mental image of an act in its execution, perhaps the reason for this is that we have sought it in habitual automatism. Let us concede that the role of the mental image comes to an end at this point. Perception of a given situation has taken over. The pianist no longer needs to imagine the movements of his fingers because perception of the notes now suffices to regulate them, whereas this was not true at the start of his musical education. One must therefore study the role of the mental image in relation to new adaptations. How does contemporary psychology envisage this problem?

The idea of individual adaptation implies that the consequences, whether good or bad, useful or harmful, react on the behavior that produced them and modify it in a way that is helpful to the individual. But in order to become the cause of an act, the consequences must precede, not follow, it. This difficulty may be resolved by noting that the effects of a first act, merely imagined mentally, precede the actual execution of a second act and can therefore modify it. But one always encounters the same problem: How is it possible to attribute results essentially different from those of original perceptions to mental images, to secondary states? To resolve the problem, we will have to accept the existence of sensations, primary states capable of reproducing or arresting the acts that caused them in the first place. Yet this power is attributed precisely to affective sensations and therefore to the memory of them. This statement requires closer examination.

Let us first consider the actual adaption to a given situation, and then the effects of subsequent repetition on the interposing adaptation.

Any object that comes into contact with a newborn infant's lips produces sucking movements. (Later, the infant will put into its mouth all the objects that come in contact with its hands or that it sees and grasps.) But sucking in turn produces variable gustatory sensations: a sweet, pleasant taste reinforces or sustains the sucking reaction; a bitter, disagreeable taste inhibits these movements and gives rise to others that are part of an antagonistic function (expulsion of the object). The original reaction to contact is thus at times stimulated, at others arrested by the development of the affective consequences. But this result is based on the existence of a preformed coordination between tastes and positive or negative motor responses localized within the function itself, the exercise of which caused these sensations in the first place. The sensations therefore confirm or inhibit the initiation of movements through an ordinary tactile sensation. What we have here is the superimposition of two cycles of preformed reactions.

Now let us suppose that the experiments are repeated and associative memory comes into play. Certain elements of the perceived situation become, through anticipation, regulators of the function. The tactile, and above all the visible, qualities of the sweet or bitter object which have always indicated corresponding taste reactions will coincide with their effects; the movements of seizing, or bringing to the mouth, and of sucking will be either confirmed or inhibited. There will be anticipation, expressed by movements of the tongue and salivary reaction in the one instance, and by a reaction of disgust in the other. Similarly, the young chicks studied by Morgan peck at all kinds of small objects (innate reaction of visual origin) and then, depending on the taste of the objects, they will either reject or swallow them (second innate reaction of gustatory origin). Influenced by experience, the chicks continue to pick up and immediately swallow grains and insects, whereas they no longer pick up certain yellow and black-striped caterpillars that have a repulsive taste. When they see such caterpillars, the chicks make a vague gesture of wiping their beaks (transference phenomena).

But all learning cannot be reduced to this pattern. Sensations that have affective value and occur in more complex adaptations produce responses that do not always have immediate repercussions on the causes of these sensations in such a precise and efficient manner as to activate or reduce them. Only under the normal conditions created by certain special instincts can one rely on the efficiency of such sensations. In general we may certainly say that the so-called pleasant sensations are characterized by the predominance of positive reactions, whereas the so-called unpleasant ones mainly bring about antagonistic actions or arrested movements. But always involved are special movements that are related to the particular quality of the sensations and the ordinary circumstances in which the sensations occur. The movements would quickly cease to exist if these sensations were the result of new situations that occur in a complex and indirect way. I pull my hand away if I feel a prick; the response is effective if the object that pricked me is stationary, but not if the prick is the result of a thorn that remains in the flesh or of an insect that is following the movements of my hand, etc. If an infant enjoys shaking an object he holds in his hand, one can maintain that the sensations he experiences directly sustain this rhythmic activity and cause him to repeat the movements. But if, in the course of this activity, a pleasant sound is heard (for example, when P at the age of six months unwittingly started the bleating of his mechanical lamb), the stimulating effect on the child's activity is not sufficient to cause him to reproduce the precise gesture that released the sound. The child will achieve this only by experimentation. It is not easy to predict how successful he will be or how long it will take him, especially if the situation involves relations with infinitely variable external objects.

In other words, adaptation, if it takes place, occurs by means of the process portrayed by Morgan and Jennings, which they described in the now classic phrase "trial and error."

IV

The Principle of Trial and Error. This theory has not always been interpreted in the same way. It does not necessarily imply the vitalist interpretation which Jennings himself seems to have rejected, nor is it some mysterious improvisation free from the laws of determinism. The "trials" are hereditary or habitual responses. Upon arriving in an area where an acid has been diffused, a protozoan draws back and turns to whichever side is appropriate because of its asymmetrical structure, and this causes it to change direction somewhat. Another forward movement takes it to the vicinity of the source of excitation. This same cycle of reactions keeps recurring until the animal, having been carried in a direction that no longer exposes it to the power of the stimulant, continues unimpeded on its way. In this instance, the organism reacts by identical responses whose accumulated effect finally liberates it. In other instances, a prolonged or repeated excitation will produce, through demand phenomena or internal change, stemming from the first ineffective reactions, a whole series of qualitatively differentiated responses which, moreover, are preformed within the animal's organism.

Here we have, it seems to me, a general law on the activity of animals at every level of mental life. An animal that is starving, enclosed in a cage and trying to get out to reach food that has been placed outside the cage, or one that cannot reach it through a direct route but must, for instance, make more or less complicated detours through a maze, finds the solution through trial and error. The first animal attempts to slip through the bars, gnaws on them, scratches the ground, etc. In other words, it responds to the situation with instinctive or habitual acts in the course of which it accidentally manages to release the liberating mechanism. The second animal wanders around, hesitates, retraces its steps, and ultimately finds the way out. Each of its responses creates a new situation and modifies its internal situation through the affective reactions it develops. The animal, therefore, seems to be behaving haphazardly, which merely means that its responses are not adapted to the problem confronting it. The fortuitous nature of the solution, moreover, is more or less pronounced, depending on the kinds of attempts made. The more experienced the animal, the more likely it is to recognize in the new problem the suggestive data of familiar acts.

Finally, in higher organisms the effects of memory — in other words, the law of transference — make themselves felt and produce not momentary adaptations but lasting changes in behavior. Movements followed by unpleasant sensations increasingly tend to become arrested before their affective consequences have had time to develop, whereas efficient movements in the end become reinforced as soon as they appear. A comparison of the successive trails followed by an animal in a maze provides a good illustration of this kind of learning. The wide-ranging vacillations so frequent at the start decrease and give place to a winding curve that tends to straighten out as the apprenticeship progresses. As it becomes more stabilized, the act no longer gives the impression of hesitation and experimentation. Certain characteristic details of the situation finally become direct signals for definitive reactions.

It is in the course of the learning process that we must seek, in man, the possible role of the *mental image* of an act or its effects. We must concede that of and by itself the memory of an interesting experience is not efficient save for the perception it represents, although much less energy is present. If we turn back to the case of instinctive adaptations mentioned earlier we may infer that memory will help to stimulate the act that reproduces the corresponding sensation. Memory of the taste of a piece of candy may stimulate movements of the tongue in a child and make "his mouth water" as if it were the taste of the candy itself. But this will not occur in most cases of new and complex adaptations. Recollected and anticipated pleasure tends to incite activity in much the same way that experienced pleasure does, that is, to arouse generally inadequate responses among which the response that reproduces the sensation may reappear. Here the attitude takes shape in a *search* for the result which one does not know how to reproduce. The idea of the result is important because of its emotional coefficient; it is not specifically related to the requisite innervation. Although this idea does not directly orient movements, it nonetheless insures their selection. It enables one to compare what one has wanted to do with what one actually does, and to judge how the accomplished act compares with the imagined one. But one should not assume the existence of an inevitable law governing progress. Memory of the act directs the deliberate reproduction of the act, just as work and concentration further discovery; they never make discovery necessary, because a discovery can only be made through lucky accidents that stem from an unstable and delicate determinism which is extremely difficult to understand.

Memory: Its Function and Forms. What forms does memory's function assume? Psychology began the study of memory with the concept of the mental image, concentrating primarily on the exceptional cases in which memory presents an independent picture, a virtual duplicate of the original perception (Taine). Then attention was focused on the recognition of objects. It was observed that the dimensions of recognitive memory are considerably more extensive than those of imaginative memory. People have described the feeling of something that is missing, of change or of the identity of a given object, although it was impossible to imagine the object until they saw it again. There are also descriptions of negative or generic memory, of the resistance of the thing forgotten to false suggestion (Abramowski). But these forms of latent memory correspond to practical attitudes: the quest for an object not clearly visualized; the striving for an end not initially envisioned but which will be recognized more or less definitely when, through trial and error, one hits upon it. A whole series of hesitant impulses, either quickly arrested or continuing apathetically, suddenly gives way to the sharp impetus of the rediscovered original act. Thus the influence of the memories inspired by individual experience can make itself felt without any precise imaginative anticipation. We are working on a mental model that is blurred or entirely obscured. Memory perfects itself by the accidental achievement of the result which is *recognized* as tallying with the model.

It is mainly in the child that there is every reason to presume that the action of memory is latent. His perceptions are filled with memories, but it is extremely difficult for these memories to become explicit, independent images. The child recovers the ball he played with a few days before and recognizes it. That is, he smiles, grasps it, and hugs it in his arms, but remains puzzled. Accidentally, he lets it fall. It rebounds; then there is fresh, more precise recognition, which culminates in another happy accident or in the intervention of another person, whom the child often asks to help in his search even while he shows, some-times quite firmly, that he can recognize what he is looking for and that he cannot be fooled. In this instance, it is no more necessary to assume the existence of a precise anticipatory image than to acknowledge or brush aside the name of the person we are seeking.

Finally, we come to the efforts inspired by the so-called image of the end in view. This image, we must remember, remains in our consciousness as a controlling process that permits the selection of movements but does not, at first, regulate their production. We are so accustomed to seeing a wish or the mere idea of an act followed by its execution that we find it difficult to realize how very indirect this causality is. It is also difficult for us to realize how it manages to establish itself. At first, however, the idea has only a causality of sorts. Because of its efficiency it tends to stimulate various forms of activity and calls into play the mechanism of trial and error; but it does not as yet possess the power to determine the performance of a differentiated act. It is quite possible to desire a movement that one does not know how to execute. To be sure, classical psychology makes a distinc-tion between will and desire. It claims that we can desire but not will an event that does not depend on us. But such a distinc-tion has meaning only for an adult, and an educated adult, at that. Many people imagine that their will has a direct effect on their health, on other people, and on external events. But it is primarily the child who has the greatest difficulty in distin-guishing those things that are dependent on him alone. His real power is very limited. He expects those who take care of him to satisfy all his desires, to remove every cause for discomfort, to place a desired object within his reach, and even to pick him up and move him. In children, all desire is first of all diffuse dynamogenesis — desire-emotion rather than desire-tendency. Even considerably later, desire is defined only insofar as it is directed toward the acts of others. Not until the process of motor education begins, only as certain mental images of acts *acquire* the efficiency that they were far from possessing in the beginning, does the notion of personal power gradually take shape. The ideomotor automatism which characterizes what we call will is, as Dumas has demonstrated, an acquired automatism.

The imaginative anticipation of the end to be achieved, moreover, exerts a very important influence on the experimentation that leads to the attainment of this end. Indeed, it is altogether possible that the experiments which precede the lucky act, recognized only when it has been achieved, can continue for a long time without coming to an end, and that the search may very well deviate from its purpose because of interesting diversions along the way. The mental image brings greater continuity to the effort and reduces trial and error because, in the very course of these experiments, it permits a comparison between what one has done and what one wishes to do. It produces actions that arrest or reverse earlier efforts, depending upon which brings one *further away from* the imagined purpose, or equally early confirmations of those movements that bring one *closer to* it. This comparison applies to the detail of forms, to the phases of movements, not merely to the result as a whole. Recognitive memory can only say yes or no to each experiment; imaginative memory can analyze the model and the copy, and correct the mistakes as they occur.

What will this learning process produce? We can predict the answer by applying the general principle of recurrence. The instigating idea of the experiments in the end becomes the instigator of the act itself, as the experiments become increasingly limited and culminate more directly in the proper solution. The instigating idea becomes a cause, or rather a component of the cause, together with the perceived situation, which governs the execution of the act. This causality, which was thought to be primitive and direct because the imagined act resembles the real act, is actually acquired by contiguity.[1] Its power is real only in regard to acts learned in this way; that is, acts in which perception of a real model (or the memory of a psychic one) directs the process of motor education. Moreover, although the mental image can always eventually be used to direct the act, the role of the image will become blurred as habit is perfected. This is why, under normal circumstances, we are so rarely aware of evoking the image. New signals are substituted for it — verbal perceptions or images, regulatory perceptions of objects, proprioceptive perceptions of earlier movements. All these are variable elements with chain reactions that thereafter will include the act.

Example. To make this discussion concrete, we might swiftly review one example. Let us choose an indubitably acquired habit — balancing oneself on a bicycle — and let us try to explain it according to the laws of transference and experimentation.

We know that this is a matter of a precarious balance maintained by continuous adjustment in steering. We might begin with the following instruction: "Turn the handlebars in the direction toward which you feel the bicycle is tilting." Here, movement conforms to a verbal and sometimes a visual image. This is the result of a much earlier process of motor education. As a determining signal, the new education substitutes the actual sensation of falling for the earlier and already efficient image.

Another method consists in avoiding falls by means of movements the instructor himself makes on the handlebars. The pupil feels both a tendency to fall and a passive inclination to

1. Thorndike, *Animal Intelligence*, p. 263: "Not that is like it, but that has gone with it."

EXAMPLE   21

avoid it, and he soon learns to take an active part in correcting the imbalance. (The same method is used in training airplane pilots.) Here the learning process consists in substituting for the motor suggestion of the passive movement, which has long been obeyed by the subject, the signal for the sensation of falling.

Until now we have been dealing exclusively with simple transference. The mechanism of trial and error intervened only secondarily, to perfect the scope of movements rather than their nature or direction. But children who are adroit can, by gliding on one pedal, learn to ride a bicycle without the help of an instructor. While playing, every child learns to balance himself on a scooter, which of course is a much easier feat. They seem to teach themselves by watching other children. But an idea derived from a model will not in itself suffice. It is impossible to learn how to balance oneself to avoid falling by observation alone. Observation can only suggest a desirable result; it cannot provide adequate knowledge of how to maintain body equilibrium. This a child discovers by trial and error. He will have to make a choice of movements in order to find those that help him keep his balance. But all this learning does not go beyond the subconscious level. A child who has mastered bicycle riding will be at a loss to answer the question: "If the bicycle tilts to the right or left, how do you keep your balance on it?"

This example clearly demonstrates the nature of progress. Earlier and earlier the organism discerns the cues to which it must respond. It reacts to the scarcely perceptible dangers of falling, whereas in the beginning it reacted only to the fall itself. We can also see the role played by mental images. If the first method is used, images or sensations are interposed that have become effective because of earlier habits; economy is related to the time needed to substitute a new signal for the old. As for the second method, when the instructor gives the signals by steering, the initial image, which reflects only the result, is but the beginning of efforts and experiments that it later stimulates and controls. It will *in the end* set the act in motion directly by associating recognized, useful movements with regulatory perceptions.

V

Kinesthetic Sensations and Images. One final question must be raised. So far we have dealt with the image of the act without specifying the concrete elements which compose it. Movement can give place to visual and auditory (word) sensations. Moreover, movement is evaluated in every instance by both superficial and profound sensitivity (kinesthetic). In psychological theories, a direct efficiency in the regulation of movement has been attributed primarily to the latter. Is there any reason to revise our thoughts on this point in the concepts discussed above?

Sensations are of major importance. First, they provide us with the knowledge of the starting position of the body and the limbs. Then, as the movement is being executed, they tell us how this is accomplished. In order to take hold of the object I see, I must feel where my hand is and sense what happens when I move it; for failing kinesthetic signals, ataxia substitutes visual signals whose automatism is less perfect and more conscious, but whose function, in principle, remains the same. In learning how to perform sleight of hand, precision exercises, or independent movements (musical fingering), one must try to really feel the movements, because each sensation governs the continuation or the correction of the movement begun. There is even a general tendency on the part of proprioceptive sensations to replace, in the regulation of habitual movements, certain extroceptive sensations which, in the beginning, intervened at every phase of the act. In writing, for example, visual sensation is thus replaced by kinesthetic sensation as groups of movements acquire internal unity and autonomy. These kinesthetic stimuli also play a role in the conscious or infraconscious regulation of associated movements. But so far there is nothing in all these facts to justify the assumption that the sensation resulting from a movement permits the latter's reproduction.

To be sure, acts often consist of a series of similar movements rhythmically repeated. Therefore the sensation of the first can become the signal for the second. Generally speaking, any perception can become the signal for any movement. But here we have a result of motor education that links the one with the other. Thus, just as the sensation produced by a movement can easily become the signal for the continuation or repetition of this movement so can it become the signal for a movement to stop and reverse itself or even to produce an ensuing movement in another member of the body.

This is quite a different matter from wondering whether, originally and primitively, independently of any special training, knowledge about the execution of a movement is the special stimulant that tends to reproduce it. If we admit that all acts are rooted in primordial instincts, then an act must first be performed as a consequence of its own stimulus before this act can be felt — unless one takes refuge in the hardly scientific, confused notion of truly fortuitous movements. And it is doubtless such a stimulus that guarantees its own repetition just as it guaranteed its initial production.

In certain cases we know something about these stimuli. They are irritations of the organs, tactile or profound. (Some examples: a child rubbing an irritated area of his body against objects; placing his hand on the irritated spot or scratching himself; reacting to organic sensations by general movements, cries, or other expressive phenomena.) Or else they are external, tactile, visual, or auditory sensations (such as adaptation and orientation of the sensory faculties, prehension, locomotion, etc.). These are, in the better known cases, the sensations responsible for motor initiatives. Kinesthetic impressions seem to intervene in the internal development of the act.

If such is the role of sensations, how are we to understand the role of kinesthetic images? Isn't it remarkable that even today their existence is questioned? It is as necessary for us to visualize the effect of our movements as is it rare for us to imagine their accomplishment in objective reality. I imagine the object that I wish to move in its new location because I want to assess the value and the possibilities of the result. But why should I imagine the sensations I will feel as I move it? In actuality I probably never imagined them, if my action derived from such instinctive reactions as prehension and locomotion that were originally subordinate to visual and tactile stimuli.

It is true, of course, that all our movements are not regulated by objects. Often we move about for the pure pleasure of doing so (in games involving physical activity, sports, dancing, etc.). In such cases, movement is not defined in its form and origins by an external purpose; it is deliberate and continued on its own. I admit that the pleasure of such exercise may consist in part in the sensation itself, and that once it is produced it may be sought again for its own sake. But in principle, the cause of the initial impulse continues to operate for a certain length of time. The fact that exercise is felt adds to a new affective excitation, just as the child's perception of his own voice provides a fresh stimulant for the organic and effective causes of his first vocal utterance. But why should this stimulant be an immediately effective and precise cause for the reproduction of this movement? It can play such a role because it provokes the reproduction of movement for testing and controlling experiments.

Some curious observations have been made by Bair and Woodworth (79)[2] on the learning of certain deliberate, exceptional acts like twitching one ear or one toe. They note the absence of memory for the sensations felt. Learning proceeds by trial and error, by the selection of movements initially included in more general reactions.

These examples will suffice to show the equivocal and improper nature of the term motor image, which often is used for the kinesthetic image in particular. The image of the movement or of its effects through one or another of the senses in-

2. The figures in parentheses refer to the bibliography, p. 211.

volved is never a first condition of it, although it can become a cause by replacing, through training, the primitive stimulant.

In this way contemporary psychology is seeking the origins of motor activity in preformed excitomotor instincts or reactions. In the course of individual development, these instincts and reactions change when subordinated to infinitely variable signals that include both external perceptions and sensations deriving from the execution of earlier phases. The mental image of the act — whether deliberate or latent — intervenes, in turn, in the formation of habits. Because of its affective quality, it exercises the function of *initiating efforts* (which are not necessarily efficient). Because of its intellectual content, the mental image exercises a function of *control* over the movements achieved and directs their selection. Precisely because of the effect of recurrence, the mental image in the end becomes a virtual motor cause for the act imagined. But its role is limited to the *construction* of complicated acts in which each element, having become a prisoner of the combinations of which it forms a part, frees itself from the prior image that then tends to become blurred.

The Problem of Imitation. But this conception leads us to raise the psychological problem of imitation in a new way. If the mental image of my own acts is not a primitive and adequate condition for their reproduction, there is additional reason to deny this role to the perception of other people's acts. Imitation therefore cannot be, even in the simplest cases, the immediate and spontaneous phenomenon that so many psychologists have described. We can no longer be content to say — at least as regards the young child — that example operates by virtue of its similarity with the image of one's own act, which would be the act itself recommencing (since thinking about movement is the direct cause for its execution). This logic, which remains entirely valid when applied to a man who knows how to imitate, does not explain how the child learns to imitate. Instead of thinking of imitation as a primitive fact, we will study its mechanism. The problem is closely related to the origin of the deliberate act; invariably involved is a real or mental model which must serve as a control for experiments before it becomes a direct cause. But this controlling function must be within the realm of the possible. In studying vocal imitation, we will try to demonstrate that it is possible in the simplest cases wherein the child can immediately identify his own acts with those of the model.

But in generalizing about the problem, we encounter more complex cases in which it is difficult to understand how the child can recognize the similarity or difference between the copy and the original and correct his first attempts. Here the function of control itself is indirect and seems to result from a rather complex learning process. Such are the problems I intend to raise. Stimulated by contemporary theories about the psychological conditions of movement, this study of imitation will perhaps contribute an experimental confirmation of the general views discussed in this first section.

VOCAL IMITATION

I

The Affective Stimulus. Greater interest has been shown in the speech of the child than in his movements. As we shall see, the problem of imitating the voice is simpler than that of imitating acts visually perceived. There are two reasons why I begin this study with an examination of this less complicated problem.

To what extent should we regard the spoken word as instinctive? Today this question can be asked only about elementary sounds, not about complex verbal combinations. Nevertheless, we must pinpoint it further.

Preformation might first of all pertain to the relation between motor groupings and organic, affective stimuli. Vocal reactions, influenced by a general state composed of emotions and needs, are a commonplace. Initially, the infant's cry expresses suffering, physical pain, and hunger; later, it expresses unpleasant emotional impressions. At the close of the second month one can distinguish cries that are symptomatic of desire, impatience, disappointment. Later, other vocal reactions will develop that correspond to a sense of well-being and pleasant stimulation. But these do not appear separately; they form part of a complex of reactions that are affective in nature. From the end of the first month to the beginning of the third, they are often accompanied by great physical effort (movement of arms and legs, head thrown back, eyebrows raised or puckered, etc.).

For each spontaneous phoneme Stern (68) tried to find a relationship to a particular orientation of the affect. His theory is based on an extensive documentation about the *lallwörter* of children belonging to different linguistic groups. First he calls attention to universal expressions of pleasure and pain by means of repeated vocalic sounds; then he divides consonants into two groups: occlusive resonant, *m*, *n*, and explosive, *b*, *p*, *d*, *t*. The first responds to a centripetal direction of attention (expression of desire, hunger), the second to a centrifugal direction (toward objects of the external world); the dental consonants, *t*, *d* have a less energetic quality (to show) than the labial consonants *b*, *p* (to reject).

Regardless of what this experiment may show, the fact that the first vocal utterances are independent of auditory data is evident from our observation of the children who are deaf at birth. Even they make vocal utterances. It is very difficult to diagnose deafness during the first months.

The direct influence of the affective state on the vocal organ is not expressed solely in the infant's cries. It is perhaps the natural root of differentiated language. The famous Laura Bridgeman, who was deaf, dumb, and blind, recognized her familiars by uttering a special sound for each person. It is said that there were about forty persons whose presence she acknowledged in this way. Her simple vocal language preceded even the gesticulated "language" she used to indicate recognition.

The Auditory Stimulus: The Theory of Instinct. Thus, affective causes can act directly, without imitation, on the vocal powers. But students differ about the vocal instinct. It can be argued that what is preformed is the subordination of the voice to the auditory stimulus. In that case, imitation itself would be instinctive. Le Dantec (39) has given this hypothesis its most radical expression. According to him, the larynx and the ear together constitute a single system because of the hereditary nerve connections which unite them anatomically. Like a phonograph, this system is composed of a receptor organ and a motor organ closely linked. Hearing is akin to the imprint of the record, which regulates the production of registered sound. Of course, this is merely illustrative. What is involved is not a mechanical process but reflexes produced by a complicated network of nerves. In certain birds, the characteristic song of the species is sung spontaneously by the young (probably under the direct influence of organic stimuli). In other species, the song is heard only when a new stimulus provided by the auditory model is added. Finally, among singing and talking birds, the influence of this new stimulus becomes so preponderant that the birds are able to learn a song that is not characteristic of their species. It is possible to learn without going outside the realm of instinct because the vocal inflections of the auditory register depend on hereditary nerve connections.

Le Dantec applied his theory to human speech. "In the child there is a consonance (necessarily hereditary) between the centripetal nerve connections of the phonating instrument and the receiving instrument; in other words, when the child says '*papa*,' he hears *papa*, thanks to one or the other of the centripetal systems. It is this hereditary consonance that makes the ensemble of these two instruments an organ that imitates sound. Because of this consonance, the child can learn to talk."

As we can see, what is involved here is a preformed connection between organs for auditory and kinesthetic receptions that result from the articulation of an identical sound. The author even says that the two sensations, "although not to be confused with one another, are at least in harmony with one another." And, as we have seen, he emphasizes the innate character of this relationship. He goes as far as to declare that the deaf mute who has learned to talk "hears" by means of his kinesthetic sensations, so that if he could be made really to hear he would at once be familiar with his new sensations.

Are we to take these statements literally? The idea of an innate relationship between the two categories of sensory properties is rather confusing. Does this add up to a kind of physiological synesthesia? The author is apparently thinking more in terms of a correlation between auditory receptions and the motor reactions necessary to produce the corresponding sounds. But, influenced by the dominant theory, which pictures kinesthetic sensations as the special stimulus of movement, Le Dantec cannot envisage the possibility of an auditory vocal command without their intervention. To put it succinctly, what he is really saying is that the child who hears a sound knows immediately how he must move his organs of articulation and phonation in order to reproduce it. He certainly learns to talk in the sense that he learns to combine sounds in order to form the words he imitates; but he does not really learn to articulate them.

Discussion. The objections one might be tempted to make to this theory are not entirely decisive. Progress in learning to speak may come slowly, but many instincts develop late, and we may mistake for learning something that is merely a spontaneous maturation of the nerve centers. Inversely, we might impute the absence of certain manifestations to a lack of experience, whereas actually it is simply due to an impoverishment of the instincts. The sensitivity of motor centers to differentiated stimuli of auditory origin may very well appear at a certain stage of organic development and disappear later. The young bird that has not heard the song of its species usually will be unable to learn it later on. These observations demonstrate how difficult it is to arrive at a negative conclusion in regard to the existence of instincts. One always tends to underestimate their importance.

Although it is best to be cautious we nonetheless believe that the role of hereditary preformation has been exaggerated and that it does not extend to the *particulars* of relations between auditory perceptions and vocal reactions.

Very early data show the role of sound as a stimulus. Auditory excitation takes its place alongside general stimuli. After his meal, sprawled on his mother's lap, freed from his diapers, or lying in the bathtub, the infant expresses a sense of well-being by making a variety of sounds. Very early *the words* of the people around him have a similar effect. For example, I noted that P uttered his first sounds (toward the end of the second month) when his mother or I talked to him for a sustained period. Similarly, L (2:15) carried on a virtual dialogue with me, babbling regularly in response to my words. P (3:21) participated in an animated conversation by great bursts of laughter. Early in the fourth month he often responded to singing or piano playing by vocal inflections devoid of any musical quality. Everyone knows how contagious crying is when several infants are in a room together,[1] and how greatly noise, especially the sound of voices, stimulates the vocal activity of children of all ages, just as it does the songs of birds in their cages.

Do these general, massive, quantitative properties of auditory sensations constitute instincts in their entirety? Should we not concede that more definite physical properties are involved — more precise relationships between auditory excitation and speech?

One can cite the following clinical fact as an argument against this idea of a more exact preformation: Among children who during the first few years of life are afflicted with right hemiplegia as a consequence of a cerebral injury, aphasia is never present. The area which we call the speech center is therefore *adapted through learning* to this function; if it should be destroyed prematurely, adaptation takes place in some other area. Consequently, there is no innate speech center (46).

Is it defensible to cite as proof of the fact that auditory-motor reactions are innate, the perfection of the child's imitation? In alluding to infantile imitation of animal sounds, Taine (71) demonstrates that the child reproduces "the guttural accents of the beasts" better than does the adult. Attempting to acquire the skill of a ventriloquist, Gutzmann was surprised to note from the very first that his two-year-old son was more adept at this than he (28). It is common knowledge that a child quickly assimilates emotional intonations, special inflections of local accents, and foreign languages. In regard to the theory we are discussing, we must remember that instinct does not consist in

---

1. However, methodical observation has shown that this contagion is not present during the first month of life (Blanton, *Ps. Review*, 1917).

a tendency to pronounce certain definite sounds (no one has ever demonstrated that there is a tendency to pronounce the sounds of spoken language by means of *ascendants*). Rather, the essence of instinct is a rigid, immediate subordination of the phonating system to the receiving system — in other words, imitation.

But does the perfection of imitation imply the existence of preformed imitator mechanisms? The answer would perhaps be yes if such perfection were achieved from the start, without trial and error. No trial is present in the first execution of a reflex. But if from the beginning perfection is achieved by means of fluctuations or progressive rectification of errors, we must look elsewhere for an explanation. Actually, we are dealing with perfectibility rather than with instant perfection. Such perfectibility is therefore only the expression of cerebral plasticity, of the capacity to *acquire* and to modify one's behavior. The situation is different for the adult. The very formation of habits, which in one way facilitates imitation, in another limits its perfectibility. Even Le Dantec has noted that a bird raised with birds of a different species and capable of imitating their song forms a habit that becomes an obstacle when it attempts to imitate the song of its own species. All the more reason then that the adult, accustomed to giving a certain letter a certain phonetic value, is hindered from giving it different phonetic values even though he might have done so had he not formed the initial habit. A child raised in an English-speaking country will have difficulty pronouncing the French *u*; he will seek some middle course between *ou* and *i* and will be at a loss to know which is best. Familiar, dependable sounds exert an attraction for the person using them; sometimes one, sometimes the other predominates. The same child, raised in France, would have no difficulty pronouncing this vowel. Should we then conclude that in the first case a preformed mechanism, linking sound with the corresponding articulation, has in some way become feeble through lack of use? Wouldn't it be simpler to admit that this mechanism never existed? One would have to repeat the same argument for each particular sound, language, and dialect because the ease with which the child imitates them, regardless of their origin, is a universal experiential fact.

In summary, upon hearing a definite sound, the adult imitates by substituting another somewhat similar sound that is familiar to him and that also does not readily lend itself to distortion. The child, although he proceeds in a basically similar fashion, as we shall see later, is far less hampered in his progress by the conjunction of other already perfect mechanisms.

We must also fix more precisely the time when the capacity to imitate sound, which we attribute a little too vaguely to the child, becomes evident. There are, of course, great individual variations; it would be difficult to establish an entirely uniform pattern. Nonetheless we can distinguish four phases:

1. During the first five months there is no evidence of imitation, if we except some very singular facts which will be mentioned later.

2. Thereafter a second period begins which is characterized both by inability to imitate, judged by the first results, and by progress achieved through continuous effort. Let us remember two remarkable facts that are hardly compatible with the doctrine of instinctive imitation. On one hand, it is very difficult for the observer to note the infant's first sounds or spontaneous vocal exercises because they are often alien to the special phonetics of our language. The close of the first year and the beginning of the second are accomplished by a considerable increase in the number of words acquired; but imitation, from a phonetic point of view, is still very inaccurate and very clumsy.

On the other hand, even during the period when the first words are uttered, there is sometimes a considerable disparity between the original and the copy. One hesitates to designate as imitation certain first attempts. We are well aware of the controversies regarding the child's "verbal creations," and at first we acknowledge the latter a little too generously. In many instances they amount to unrecognizable copies of adult words.

We also know how difficult it is for a stranger to understand a very small child. Imitated words are recognized as such within the narrow circle of the child's intimates.

3. The third period, which even in the most precocious children barely begins before sometime in the second year, is one of triumph in the area of imitation (although a good deal of progress remains to be made). This is the period of echolalia, when the child promptly repeats words heard only once, ends of sentences, etc., regardless of whether he understands them. It is the period during which he assimilates local accents quickly whenever his surroundings are changed. It is also the period when a more varied way of speaking — often rather surprising for the aptness of its emotional inflection — (P, 16 months), replaces the earlier monotonous diction.

Schäfer (58) cites a very clear example. His children, who speak *Hochdeutsch* (High German), vacationed in Franconia for two months. The elder (3 years and 3 months) began to adopt the local accent (*a* is substituted for *ei* in certain words) and used it generally. This faulty pronunciation began five or six weeks after arrival but quickly disappeared when the holidays ended. No change at all was observed in his two-year-old sister's speech. But the following year, after the family had returned, she too began to speak with the local accent. I have noticed the same thing in my children during our holidays (they are a little older than the Schäfer children). When we vacationed in eastern France, they quickly adopted the local accent (nasal speech, the *r* rolled, the vowels closed).

4. During the final phase, the influence of habit begins to clash with that of the new acquisitions: pronunciation becomes increasingly stabilized. For the school-age child, the acquisition of a double set of phonetics while learning a foreign language is difficult at best, whereas it would have been a mere game during the first few years.

All these facts are difficult to reconcile with the hypothesis of an innate, precise determinism. The auditory-motor apparatus is not the phonographic recording device Le Dantec has described. If, generally speaking, excitations of auditory origin tend to stimulate the mechanism of speech, we must look for a cause other than instinct if we are to comprehend how this determinism manifests itself.

II

Self-Imitation. It seems fitting to begin this study with what Baldwin (1) has described as self-imitation, or circular reaction. Use of the voice is first of all a reaction quite distinct from affective life. But the sensations that result from it are tactile and kinesthetic on the one hand, auditory on the other. The child will attempt to reproduce these various effects by spontaneous vocal exercises (*lallen, krähen*) that constitute the first stage in his vocal development.

These spontaneous products of the child's vocal gymnastics are extremely varied. Because it is impossible to transcribe them, we resort to the testimony of phoneticians experienced in recording the special qualities of sound. *Krähen* is described by Ronjat (57) as "that period during which can be heard all the sounds that the vocal organs are capable of reproducing in every position and variety of manner and point of application; sounds that never again are heard in the lifetime of the subject from the time he tries to reproduce what he hears being said to adults." Meringer observed in his children "a variety of whistling notes similar to those used in Slavic languages, plus palatal and nasal sounds like those encountered in African languages." "During this period," says Gutzmann (30) "there appear the clickings of Hottentots, the throaty sounds of Semitic languages, inspirated and expirated sounds, etc."

At first these sounds are not subordinate to the auditory image. Those that are the expression of affective movements never completely free themselves from them. The child does not seem to be able to reproduce them when speaking of what he thinks of such and such a sound. He plays with his voice like a novice musician who amuses himself by pounding on the keyboard, without being able to reproduce the sounds from the memory of their acoustic quality after moving his hand. This, we believe, demonstrates the inadequacy of the old notion that the child automatically creates for himself a reversible association between vocal effort and its auditory effect. If this were true, learning would result much more directly from the first vocal utterances. We believe, on the contrary, that the memory of sound becomes motor only after having directed the efforts of the child to reproduce it, and that this memory controls the result and in the end becomes its cause. In other words, so far as Baldwin's concepts are concerned, the facts correspond less to the idea of simple imitation than to that of persistent imitation, or the search for a certain effect by means of memory-controlled trial and error.

We are familiar with the tendency of children to reduplicate. In the beginning, speech is only the rather monotonous repetition of a few sounds which amount to lengthy monologues (*eu, eu, eu*). During a more advanced stage, real syllables are doubled or tripled (*papa, papapa . . . tata, coco, caca, lolo*); or else the same vowel is repeated with an interpolated consonant (*ata, apapa, adada*). Finally the same consonant is retained with variation of the vowel (*tita, atita*). Thus we come to the period when the first significant words are uttered even though the habit of reduplication persists; and we know that the infantile language marked by this kind of reduplication is not an artificial product of imitation but rather something universally imposed by the child on his surroundings.

The explanation of this phenomenon must be sought in several areas. Neuromuscular activity tends at the start to be rhythmic. Moreover, it is consistent with physiological laws to say that a system beginning to function remains more excitable, as if the effect of its activity is the overcoming of a certain inertia. It is easier to repeat than to modify the adaptation of organs. Hence, the phenomenon of assimilation which continues to produce reduplication when the child tries to pronounce disyllables. Such tendencies are evident in the adult's rapid speech whenever automatic coordination becomes inadequate. In language disturbances, stuttering and anomolies known as perseverance are somewhat akin to this.

But there are elements in reduplication other than the effects of inertia, simplification, and the tendency to make the least possible effort. To the child, the sound produced is an interesting perception that has affective value. It soon acts as a stimulant, supplementing whatever causes the first vocal utterance and quickly taking its place. More and more, this becomes a conscious game. When the child has mastered vocal utterances, he derives pleasure from the repetition of sounds; he interpolates them anywhere — hence the temporary manner of vocalizing. A new sound becomes integrated into words where it does not belong. When he was fifteen months old, P practiced imitating the final *r* and amused himself by adding it to the end of every word. He would say *peur, voir, boire,* and then papa*r* for Papa, Ame*r* for Ahmed, Po*r* for Paul. Although some of these examples can be interpreted as transcriptions of difficult sounds (but not impossible at that stage), the same cannot be said for the first (papa*r*). Bloch (6) cites similar examples (papa*t* or papa*p*). We find the same thing occurring among much older children.

The explanation of this rather paradoxical phenomenon is probably to be found in the tardy subordination of vocal reactions to auditory perceptions. From the very outset these are sounds which the child seems to have a certain difficulty imitating, and this difficulty persists for a while. An attempt has been made to establish a chronological order for the appearance of different consonants, but this poses the problem in an ambiguous fashion. Sounds such as *g, r, br, cr,* and *l,* which are present in the early utterances of children, seem to be eliminated when they speak their first words. They are either omitted or replaced by other sounds. Paul did not use the final *r* again until he was fifteen months old, after it had been replaced by an aspirated consonant or by a lengthening of the preceding vowel, and the intervocalic *r* was suppressed or replaced by an *n*. And yet all kinds of *r*'s had been present in the babblings of the first months. Even more characteristic is the *g*, which reappeared only in the seventeenth month, whereas it had been an essential part of his first utterances. Grammont believes that the infant prefers certain sounds because of the strong tactile sensations that accompany them. The infant tries to reproduce everything he hears, but especially whatever has a scratching or rolling sound — hence the expressive terms *krähen* and *lallen*.

If the infant is seeking tactile sensation, it naturally costs him a fresh effort to acquire auditory control. In the beginning, certainly, he makes many throaty sounds; later, a displacement occurs from the back of the mouth to the front, at the point of the occlusion of the air passage. Then guttural sounds are replaced by dental and labial consonants. (This is not an absolute rule; the *k* sound has never ceased to be pronounced by either of our children, although the *t* has often been substituted for it.) This phenomenon may be related to local irritation connected with teething. For three months the sounds *gh* and *rh* predominated. Then, rather suddenly, P almost ceased to pronounce them, using dental and labial consonants instead. At that time his gums were swollen and irritated. He was constantly rubbing his tongue against them or putting his tongue between his lips. And he would continuously produce a sound that cannot be transcribed: *pp* . . . *bb* . . . *ptt* . . . , his lips protruding and drops of saliva falling from his mouth. Soon he pronounced *pap, mam, ata, ada.* . . . Both children behaved in identical fashion at the same age.

We can therefore say that various sensations determine such vocal gymnastics in the beginning. Be that as it may, the exercises do help sooner or later to establish an increasingly precise auditory vocal control. However, this does not, in my opinion, settle the very controversial question of internal language. Is speech a kind of repetition of an internal voice consisting of auditory images? This is certainly true in specified instances but not perhaps in others. All kinds of substitutes can assume the role of auditory images. Usually it is the thought of the objects and of the situations that directly stimulates verbal automatism. But the auditory image plays an indispensable role in the constitution of this mechanism.

We must also state precisely in what sense this self-imitation is voluntary. In so doing, we must recall the principles established on this point in the first section. A desire for something, in the strict sense of the word, does not relate to what one knows one can obtain, because the action involved has already been mastered. The sound that attracts, once recovered, will be recognized at first, then sought again, so that the following sounds will seem to be so many failures and triumphs and the desire to imitate will gradually be affected by the very progress made in imitating.

III

First Imitations. What does the child require in order to be able to imitate the voice of *others*? Since the sound of his own voice affects his auditory organ in much the same way that an external sound does, it is conceivable that once the child's circular reaction has begun, these sounds will trigger the entire mechanism. One must take into account the fact that at the outset imitation will be possible only for those sounds which the child himself has made and which are familiar to him. Only much later do these sounds become the agents of new phonemes.

However, even in this initial form, imitation cannot be achieved for some time. This will hold true despite efforts to help by imitating the child's voice. The experiment will have a much greater chance of success if a familiar sound is produced *immediately after* the child has made it himself. I often noticed this during the fifth month when I tried to get the child to repeat the sounds most frequently made at that time (*ata, atita, tata,* etc.). Preyer (54) has conducted a number of such experiments with retarded children. Imitation, which had begun during the tenth month, was still quite imperfect by the fourteenth month. But, he goes on, "over and against these imperfect imitations, one must call attention to the parrotlike precision with which certain syllables are repeated and spontaneously pronounced by the child, syllables which I repeat to him as soon as he utters them." [2] And indeed, it is understandable that perception of someone else's speech should merely aggravate the latent tendency to repeat, which stems from the auditory perception of the first sound. The imitation of others develops as a consequence of the child's tendency toward self-imitation. At this stage of imperfect differentiation, the same is not true of an excitation, even a familiar one, that conflicts with the inertia of inactive faculties.

The same considerations also explain why a child often produces a sound different from the one he was attempting to utter. Sometimes this sound, which has been repeated in preceding experiments, is rather wide of the mark.

When does imitation begin, and what are the conditions for its development?

Within a two-week period (2:11 to 2:26), I clearly noticed in one of my children a number of imitations related to the principal sounds that were familiar to him at that time (*ghe*, *pou*, *re*). In the midst of the experiment we changed the order of the syllables. The child stared at the person talking to him (his mother or myself) and smiled. Sometimes we had to wait five or six seconds and repeat the syllable before getting a response. But there was no doubt in our minds that this was true imitation.

Thus a first test (2:11) yielded positive results with the three sounds, *ghe*, *pou*, and *re*. But P was not always disposed to respond. Three days later, when I uttered these sounds successively, they were immediately repeated. Five days later the same test was again successful; after a few minutes it was repeated again and proved successful, changing the order of the syllables. The next day two more tests were conducted with similar results (the sounds were made by P's mother), but in the second test P substituted *re* for *pou*. Three days later I noticed that although

2. Preyer, *L'âme de l'enfant*, p. 384.

these same phonemes appeared once again in a long-drawn-out, spontaneous babbling, it was difficult to get P to repeat them.

Most observers have noted the first vocal imitation at a much later age (Preyer at ten months, Major at nine months, Linder at eight). Darwin was afraid he had made a mistake when he thought he noticed it at four months. Baldwin did not observe it at all during the first three or four months. Stern (68), however, reported a test similar to ours. He noted that at two and one-half months it was possible to make the infant repeat the two first sounds of his spontaneous vocabulary (*erre, erre,* and *kra-kra*). Scupin (61) cited another example. At seven weeks his son looked at his mother attentively as she said the sounds he was in the habit of articulating spontaneously: *a, a, brr, bu.* He moved his lips, and after she repeated *a-brr* to him several times, he smiled; then, after moving his lips silently a few times, he uttered *a-brr* with great effort.

Similar observations were made by Ferretti on a three-month-old infant (24) and by Dix on a three- to four-month-old.

It is altogether understandable that such precocious imitations should go unnoticed or be considered doubtful. They are, to be sure, quite exceptional. It would be wrong to regard them as signaling a significant trend in imitation. After the above-mentioned tests had been made, my attempts to have them repeated failed. It was not until the fifth month that I was able, by concentrating on sounds that the baby had just uttered (*ata, atita,* etc.) to obtain further imitations. During that time P was imitating the noise of a kiss; then in the sixth month, another sound (*bo*). But now we had reached a new phase, that of imitating the first significant *words*.

These first "sporadic" (Stern) imitations are interesting because they demonstrate that the sensory-motor mechanism springing from circular reaction can play a role so very early. But why should progress be so slow?

The Differentiated Auditory Perception. In order to generalize about imitation, two conditions that are virtually inseparable one from the other must be met. Through the development of auditory perception, the phoneme must become a recognizable *object* of sorts despite differences in tone and pitch, and this "object" must tend to emerge as distinct from the sonorous continuity in which it appears. Furthermore, it must become an understandable sign that holds a greater interest than mere vocal noise. To repeat, the two conditions are inseparable. Perception of the phoneme is perfected at the very moment that it acquires a symbolic value. We must therefore study the development of the *differentiated auditory perception*.

The auditory sensation exists from the time the normal deafness of a newborn infant disappears. Reactions to sound occur on the fourth day. By the fifth day the head turns, as if seeking the origin of the sound. This orientation to sound, however, is very slow to develop precision. Not until the fourth month does it become rapid, regular, and dependable, permitting the infant to distinguish the voice better and to look at the face of the person who is speaking. At this time, differentiated perception of language begins. It will pave the way for the powerful tendency to imitate that typifies the end of the first year and the beginning of the second.

The fact that the recognition of words precedes their enunciation in both spontaneous and imitated speech is evident from the reactions which the words reflect.

During the second and third months it becomes plain that attention is being paid to definite sounds. Among the indicators are the cessation of certain activities, facial expression, smile, etc. It is clear from the baby's attitude that familiar voices are now recognized even when the person is not seen (L, 2:13; P, 3:2). The word *papa* was recognized by L in her second month, by P in his fourth month (3:15). Upon reaching the fourth month, came *Paulic* (for Paul), *nurse, the other* (meaning the other breast); in the fifth month: *mama, big brother*. Now we begin to play games in which the baby responds to gestures, mimicry, and voices. Soon the voice alone comes to play the preponderant role. Speech suffices to play a game; there is no longer any need to mime or gesticulate. The baby knows a little song whose last verses make him laugh. Gradually we notice that he anticipates the laughter as soon as the preceding verses are sung. He waves his hand when someone says *Good-bye*! and raises himself with his arms when we say *Dancing*! *one, two, three*! (L, 5 months). L also reacts appropriately to the following commands: *Hug*! *Pull the beard, the hair*! *Do the puppets*! (Imitate a song called "Les Marionnettes"). L looks right at the person or object when she is asked: *Where is papa*? *big brother*? *Raymond*? *the bottle*? *the fire*? *the kitty*? *daddy*? *the dish*? She reacts to the following with appropriate effort (we help whenever necessary): *Come*! *Sit*! *Stand up*! And also when we speak of going *"néner"* (baby talk meaning going for a walk — *promener*) or ask her: *Be the little old lady*! or *She's so pretty*! etc. It should be said that these words, at first recognized when uttered by a particular person, are now understood when others say them. The meaning of the verbal symbol has become independent of the tone or pitch of the voice or of any special inflection, and of the doubtless multiple circumstances with which it was initially associated.

As for progress in the auditory perception of words, only a few word sounds are imitated until the infant reaches its seventh month. Although L understood the word *papa* at the age of three months, she did not enunciate it until the seventh month, when she was also saying *tata*, *tété*, and *man*. These four words constituted the entire vocabulary of both infants at the age of six months. However, it is also clear to us that these four words represent but a very small part of the total vocabulary already understood at that time. We will see, as we pursue our study through the second half of the infants' first year, that this disparity increases. Our problem will be to estimate accurately the size of the vocabulary understood.

In Preyer's child (54), who was very slow to speak, a "unilateral communication through speech" was established between the twelfth and the eighteenth months. The child understood a good many words but spoke very little and was able to repeat what he heard only quite haphazardly (*papa* was repeated for the first time during the second year), although his father frequently practiced vocal exercises with him. A few words of the child's spontaneous vocabulary were obviously the result of imitation. During the seventeenth month he was able to distinguish the following words one from another despite their somewhat similar sounds:

Uhr Schuh Stinn Nase Bart   Heiss   Schulter
Ohr Stuhl   Kinn   Blasen Haar Fleisch   Fuss

With the exception of *Heiss*, the infant had not as yet repeated any of these words.

Stern (68), who uses the term "language comprehension" in a rather narrow sense, observed that a slight disparity exists between the first words understood and the first words spoken. But from the time the two functions are operating, progress in speech becomes slower than progress in comprehension. At the age of a year and three months, one of Stern's children understood three times more words than he spoke. At a year and six months, this disparity was even more pronounced. By the time the child was a year and eight months, it was impossible to estimate the number of words he understood.

The same is true in regard to music. L's reactions to the song, "*Les Petites Marionnettes*," preceded by two months her first attempts to imitate it. In this instance I made sure through verification that the song was recognized without the help of gestures or word (L, 6:15).

In summary, then, differentiated auditory perception — which can be measured on the basis of the child's behavior — always precedes speech: it is a prerequisite of imitation and remains subordinate to its progress. Moreover, the two functional developments, language comprehension and progress in auditory perception, are inseparable. Words do not possess for the child solely a sensory, musical interest; rather, he usually selects those words that are significant to him. Progress in imitation cannot precede the development of intelligence. It is not enough that a function becomes possible; its exercise must respond to a motive. Pure parrotlike repetition does not suffice to nurture imitation.

The Verbal Impulse. But that is not all. The symbolic significance of the words is not enough to insure the development of speech. In certain children, the disparity between comprehended and spoken language remains even greater. Some understand everything but do not speak spontaneously for a very long time, following which speech comes rather suddenly (21). Others receive artificial training (like that given to the deaf and dumb). Often such children are thought to be deaf and dumb, yet they react to speech, obey verbal commands, point to objects named, and in other respects as well do not always behave like defective children. These facts concerning the normal and abnormal disparity between language comprehension and speech reduce to its proper perspective the often expressed idea that the habit of speech, because of some kind of motor accompaniment, makes discrimination possible in auditory perception. Doubtless one should regard this notion as an exaggeration of a sound idea.

Abnormal disparity and, in some extreme cases, the consequent muteness which accompanies it in the absence of local physical causes (adenoids, tonsilitis) stem from a general or special kind of laziness. This often coincides with a parallel slowness in learning to walk. The child will have to be stimulated to walk and talk; he will have to be made artificially to feel the pleasure in playing with words which the normal or precocious child experiences and which the instinct to learn tends to promote. The first words one addresses to a child are invitations not only to perceive, to pay attention, to react, but also to utter words. We encourage a child's initiative in many ways (caresses, laughter, signs of approval); this is clearly apparent not only in regard to his first words but also to their accepted meaning. Retarded speech is a phenomenon related to mental and physical passivity; its occurrence depends not only on the child's general intellectual vitality but also on his nature, his tendency to assert himself and to participate (as an observer more than as an actor) in social life. This reinforces our notion that verbal imitation is an activity that demands an effort rather than a purely automatic response.

Constructive Imitation. We have seen that imitation is initially related to the sounds with which the child has familiarized himself through his own vocal exercises. At what point does imitation become educative, causing new sounds to be produced that are alien to the child's spontaneous vocabulary? This question is not nearly as simple as it might seem at first.

Several authors have attempted to record the first imitation of a new word. It is not easy to contrast and compare their data. Some writers note the moment when all one has to do is to utter a word in the presence of the child for him to repeat it correctly. Others call attention to spontaneous and capricious imitations, or to imitations that are consistent with marked distortions of the word. For example, Preyer (54) notes the first utterance of a new word at fifteen months; and yet, as early as the eleventh month, it is possible to make out the child's name, distorted, of course, in a spontaneous combination of sounds (Akkee Prayer for Axel Preyer). Moreover, it is very difficult to be sure that the sound is new. No one can claim to have an accurate record of the spontaneous babbling by means of which the child practices speaking, and which continues to play a rather important role for quite a while (L, up to 16 months). On the other hand, should we classify as imitation the first "dialogues" in which, characteristically enough, infants respond without any really recognizable words but with the proper intonations (the voice falling at the end of sentences, the narrative and interrogatory tone)? These dialogues contrast markedly with the monotonous diction of the early months (end of the first year).

The Influence of Prior Acquisitions. A further complicating factor is that imitation, after a certain length of time but probably rather early, ceases to be a direct copy of the model. The child is imitating *by memory*. When a word or a new sound appears, it is very difficult to tell which perception served as the model. Often, very early impressions are involved. These reveal themselves very tardily through the control they exert on the first attempts at talking. Newer impressions tend to be less powerful. A case in point is the child raised by an Italian nurse-maid. As he began to talk a month after the nurse's departure, he mixed Italian phonetics with the French vocabulary learned from his parents.

Problems due to the infant's vocal "creations" and which result from imitation challenge us to discover how differentiation, the gradual correction of these first attempts, is achieved. Efforts to conform to an external model do not differ essentially from those that lead to the reproduction of an accidental sound through self-imitation. You repeat to the child the word he pronounced badly; you thereby perfect and reinforce auditory memory. In this way errors are gradually eliminated and a selection made of those movements that have produced a result similar to one's memory of it. The new words, once acquired, will be subject to many subsequent fluctuations, but ultimately they will become fixed through fresh and continuing confirmations. The distinctive feature of imitation is greater interest in the model. The word has more prestige value than spontaneous productions because of its association with an action or a person. It is likewise distinguishable from the changing and ephemeral sounds produced by babbling because it does not fluctuate. Like all other social phenomena, imitation of others is a *discipline*. In the first verbal utterances there is of course a desire to produce a definite sound; but it is capricious, devoid of stability or perseverance, occurring before the influence of social conformity makes itself felt.

At first the model sound serves solely as a control, and ineffective efforts at imitation will provoke those habitual reactions that most resemble the model.

At six months L had not yet imitated a single word. But in the course of her continuous babbling, she uttered a lengthy

series of sounds — *ta ta ta* . . . , *dada da*. . . . These in turn
determined her choice of the words to be imitated and influenced the way in which she distorted them. The first word
uttered was *téter*, "to nurse," usually distorted to sound like
dédé (beginning of the seventh month). The cry of the lamb,
bê, became *dé* (generic word for all quadrupeds). One day she
tried to say her own nickname and produced *Tet* for Zette.
Many actions were accompanied by *dé, da, dida*, which then
became *dom* (an expression which to her meant *donne* ("give"),
but which she also used in a broader sense — *dada* (*cheval*,
"horse") *dédé*, her personal distortion of *dodo* (to sleep, in
French baby talk), *dadame* (*la dame*, the lady) — all of which
were part of the same series of babblings.

Papa (at eight months), one of the first words uttered, opened
another series of babblings: *pas, a pas* (negation) *pépée* (*pou-
pée*, "doll"), *pipi*, "wee-wee" — *papo* (*chapeau*, "hat"), (*papier*,
"paper"), etc.

Similarly, *bonbon* ("candy") (tenth month) became *ba ba,
ban-ban* — *bobo* ("hurt"), *bon* ("good"), etc. And again, *nénin*
("nipple"), or *nin-nin* (eight months), a word with many meanings, became *maman, main-main, main* ("hand"), *ama*, and
mamamm (*fromage*, "cheese") and then *néné* (*promener*, "take
a walk"), *nini* (*enfant*, "baby"), etc.

Thus very different meanings attach to these vocal sounds
which the child prodcces more or less in the same way. Not
until later is he able to sort them out, although he certainly
does perceive the differences between the words which he has
in mind and is clumsily trying to imitate.

When words are imitated immediately, it is clear that they
formed part of the sounds of an earlier vocabulary and that
they are distorted as a consequence of assimilation with familiar
sounds. This is true for *ati* (*assis!* "sit down") and *ata* (*à table*
"dinner's ready"), which L repeated (twelve months) after hearing it only once, but which were part of the spontaneous vocal
exercises of that period (*ati, ata, atita*, etc.).

Similarly, P (twelve months) grouped many words around a

few sounds between which he seemed scarcely to have differentiated:

1. *Pa* (papa), *pain-pain* ("bread"), *papo* (*chapeau*, "hat"),
papou (*sa soupe*, "soup"), *popo* (*pot*, "pot" or *pomme*, "apple");

2. *Bain* ("bath"), *ba* (*balai*, "broom") *bo* (*brosse*, "brush"),
bou, mba or *aba* (*embrasser*, "hug");

3. *Maman, nin-nin, gnian-gnian, néné*. . . . Initially, it was
almost impossible to tell the difference between *pain-pain,
papa, papo*.

These series later evolved in such a way that words like *ba*
designated successively: *le balai* ("broom"), *le bas* ("stocking"),
là-bas ("over there"), *la boîte* ("box"), *la banane* ("banana"),
le bois ("wood"), etc. And notice the influence of *a pu* (*il n'y en
a plus*, "there's no more") on *a peu* (*il pleut*, "it's raining"), *a
pou* (*la poule*, "chicken").

A newly acquired word, *tape*, reacted on *papo* (*chapeau*,
"hat"), which had been learned earlier, and transformed it into
tapo (thirteenth month); *cop-cop* (*coupe-coupe*, "cut," scissors)
influenced the baby's imitation of *ça pique* ("that pricks"),
which became *kip-kip* or *kik-kik*, etc.

Thus, accompanying the model immediately presented — the
word heard or the person the child is remembering — is the influence of familiar sounds; the first sound is recalled because
of its resonance. In infant imitation, these two influences are
combined. The perception or image is precise; but there is quite
a disparity between differentiating in order to react correctly
to a word, for example, and differentiating in order to be able
to reproduce it. The latter implies an interplay of special habits.

To return once more to the problem raised in the preceding
chapter: Why is progress in imitation so slow? It is slow because
it implies the capacity of auditory perception to differentiate,
and this in turn is linked, to some extent, with the understanding of language, which is the purpose of imitation. A second
reason is that imitation is dependent on a desire to talk which
needs to be stimulated. In order to account fully for the disparity between the two functional developments, we must add

that the readiness to imitate, and to a certain extent the awareness of being able to imitate, *are functions of the richness of
already acquired speech.* And this results from the role which
we have just attributed to earlier habits. In the beginning, the
distance is sometimes so great that one would hesitate to say
that there is any intention to imitate; yet already the speech of
others has begun to stimulate the child's speech. In the end
(the third year), the child produces a new word immediately,
and all its sounds are familiar to him because they were present
in other words that formed part of his vocabulary. Meanwhile,
each new sound that he masters remains initially a distortion
of earlier acquisitions. The more meager the vocabulary the
fewer resources it provides for imitation, which will come tardily
if it is attempted at all.

Imitation is therefore not the simple phenomenon discussed
by Le Dantec. It is a transposition, a translation of what the
child hears, in phonetics that are familiar to him. The best
way to describe a child's imitation of language is to compare
it to his drawings. He transposes the model, using the symbol
that he knows how to reproduce (this is a man, a head, a hand)
and forever trying to reduce to a minimum the effort to copy
accurately. As soon as the symbol is understood and accepted
by those around him, it fulfills its functions. Similarly, at a
later stage, the child (and also the adult who is not well educated) remains incapable of reproducing accurately the word
he hears. He transposes it, believing he is repeating it. Likewise, the bilingual child (57), reporting to his German-speaking
mother the words of his French-speaking father, shows no clear
awareness of this bilingualism.

The Correction of Imitation. So we might say that basically
the difference we had previously established between the way
an adult and a child imitate is not very great; it amounts merely to a difference in degree. The influence of habit and the
pull of previous learning constitute from the start both a help
and a hindrance. In the child, the first role predominates; in

the adult, the second. Besides, the child corrects himself, especially if he is prodded not to be lazy. Grammont shows us the child trying to reproduce a sound by means of various substitutes which are for him so many attempts to reproduce a model that he cannot attain. Ronjat notes that after the sixteenth month, the hitherto well-established system of articulation is constantly being undermined by the contrast between the phonemes uttered and those heard. Occasionally, words learned during the early period remain the same; at other times, they are altered. During this period the new words tend to fluctuate, now consisting of assimilated phonemes, now of phonemes pronounced as they had been during the earlier phase. Bloch (6) demonstrates that this kind of self-correction occurs even for words actually not repeated to the child after the change in his pronunciation. What takes place is a retrospective analysis, aided by newly acquired habits, of an exact auditory memory.

Children vary in the measure and rapidity with which they follow this path. In learning to speak a foreign language, the individual ceases to correct himself either when he reaches the point at which he can be understood, or when he no longer feels exposed to ridicule or hostility; or, again, when he is so fluent that no one can tell what country he comes from. In the same way, certain children are lazy and dawdle, using the incorrect forms of childish pronunciation; others progress rapidly, perhaps because they are more sensitive to the musical quality of language, but also because they are exposed at an early age to a finer, more distinguished form of speech.

This rule applies to all the aspects of learning a language. Imitating a phrase or a combination of words is not essentially different from imitating a single word. It always involves progressive self-correction. Even before L uttered isolated words, we noticed "phrases" of a kind, accompanied by characteristic intonations. Later (twelve months), she interspersed the few words she knew in "padded phrases" with sounds indistinctly mumbled. Finally, the whole gradually took on a more correct form in which the minor words of a sentence became increasingly comprehensible. Children who, for a protracted time, speak only by using a single word, convey to others the impression that the word (sometimes limited to one syllable or to vowels) is the copy of a phrase or expression whose accentuated or familiar characteristics alone subsist, and which will be supplemented in due course as imitation becomes less inefficient.

We have pinpointed our objections to the theory based on instincts. Little by little, imitation becomes more discriminating, progressing from banal reactions to auditory perception of the human voice. The influence of the form of the sounds we have cited by way of example is at first too limited to give the observer and even the subject the sense of having achieved a satisfactory imitation of the model. The prolonged periods of trial and error by means of which speech progresses to achieve in the end its correct form demonstrate the distance that separates the two functions of the mental image: *control* and *direct regulation* of acts.

The Role of Vision. So far we have discussed auditory regulation of the voice. Let us now ask ourselves whether sight is associated with hearing in this function.

Some authors attribute a considerable role to hearing. Onufrowicz[3] states that in the beginning the infant cannot repeat a sound if it is emitted by a person standing behind him. The importance of sight is likewise apparent when we learn to pronounce a foreign language. "In order to learn to pronounce the English *th*," Onufrowicz points out, "the sound is not enough. We have to *see* where the tip of the tongue should be in relation to teeth and lips." The first words an infant learns are always those that require obvious, easily observable movements of the lips (papa, mama). As early as 1768, Pereire had noted that these words could be learned spontaneously by infants who were deaf-mutes at birth. Gutzmann (28) also remarked that it is easier to understand an address when one can see the face of the speaker. If we have any difficulty hearing

3. According to Leroy, *Le langage*, p. 40.

the words at the opera, we need only to peer through our opera glasses and see the singer's face to rectify the situation at once. It has also been said that hearing (29) unaided by sight results in an imperfect impression of words. This is apparent not only from the mistakes made by stenographers but also from Gutzmann's experiments in telephonic communication in which proper names and syllables that made no sense were used.

In the preceding discussion let us set aside the indisputable facts about the auxiliary role of visual perception in language among adults and address ourselves solely to the following question: How much of a part does the role attributed to sight play in the way a child learns to speak?

Great importance has been ascribed to the fact that very early the child watches attentively the lip movements of the person talking to him. The child's eyes are not directed toward the eyes of the other person but toward the mouth; at such times, the child often moves his lips without uttering a sound. I observed this often in P (from 3:22 to 5:8), but far less often in L. (However, I did notice this with singing [10:15].)

The following are the facts I recorded, in chronological order. (I did not omit experiments in the reproduction of sounds made by the child, which occurred around the middle of the third month.)

P 3:22. His mother clearly enunciated *pa . . . pa . . . pa. . . .* He set his lips and moved them silently.

3:24. Twice, when the word *papa* was uttered in his presence, he answered with an *a*, using the same intonation.

3:30. He responded with a variety of nonmusical vocal inflections to a song sung to him by his mother.

4 months. He made sounds while the piano was being played.

4:4. Very pronounced vocal inflection in his spontaneous babbling.

4:10. A kind of nonmusical imitation in a high-pitched voice of the song his mother was singing to him.

4:17. Silent lip movements when his mother spoke to him.

4:22. The same thing.

5:2. More definite efforts during the last few days to articulate (*a, e, ua, atita, titit*). Lip movements accompanied by whispered sounds.

5:6. Ready imitation of sounds that were repeated to him after he first tried to utter them; he stared attentively at the person who was talking to him (*ata, ta, atita*). When I said *pa* to him (he had not yet said this on his own), he stared at my lips and moved his silently.

5:9. His mouth was puckered in a grimace and his eyes were closed when, with some effort, he said *ta-tita*. He imitated the noise of a kiss by smacking his lips.

Some authors find it quite natural that the child should imitate lip movements. But although the child can compare the sound of his voice to that of the model's, is it correct to say that the child's own lip movements, which he himself has never seen, are comparable to his purely visual experience of the lip movements of the model, and that one may be patterned after the other?

Visual Imitation. Preyer, who realized the importance of this question, tried to formulate a conclusion about it by conducting an experiment. He noticed that as early as the tenth day the movements involved in protruding the lips and in pressing them together occurred *spontaneously*. He tried to verify this by bringing imitation into play. He placed himself in front of the infant and made the same movement himself. "Although the movement is a very familiar one to the child at the age of fourteen weeks, it cannot be produced by means of imitation even under the most favorable circumstances."[4] Once, at the end of the fifteenth week, the infant did produce it very imperfectly. No observations were recorded during the next few days. During the ensuing weeks, all attempts to elicit an imitation of this movement failed, and Preyer began to think that the one isolated example obtained previously might have been a coincidence. During the *seventh month*, however, there was

4. Preyer, *L'âme de l'enfant*, p. 235.

definite imitation, "and it could not be attributed to chance." The same author called attention to another instance of imitation, the act of putting the tongue between the lips (seventeenth week). By the tenth month, the infant correctly imitated all kinds of movements.

On rereading these observations carefully, we realize that even under the most favorable circumstances it is impossible during the first few months to elicit an imitative act of visual origin. The single example of an imitated lip movement in the fifteenth week seems suspect, and the author quite rightly wonders whether it should be taken seriously. The same is not true of the cited examples that occurred in the seventh and tenth months. But by then, as we have seen, the imitation of sounds begins. It is the earliest and the easiest of all forms of imitation; it is as intelligible as visual imitation is inexplicable. That the latter can prepare the way for the former may therefore be regarded as doubtful.

When the child stares at the person talking to him and watches his lip movements, he does so primarily as a consequence of the auditory reflex, which is completely established no later than three and a half to four months after birth. Thereafter this reflex controls all sounds that attract the infant's attention. It is precisely at this stage in the infant's development that we begin to notice the so-called imitation of lip movements. The infant, we may therefore conclude, does not watch the lips in order to "imitate" them; he looks in the direction from which the voice is heard and watches the mouth move. We must admit, morever, that once visual perception has been associated with auditory perception, the infant may try to watch lip movements that signal speech and thereby distinguish, just as we do, which individual among several present is speaking.

But if this is so, why does the infant move his lips, thus giving the impression that he is imitating what he sees?

It is our belief that this represents an attempt to imitate the speech which he hears, an attempt that usually fails for the reasons we have already explained. The child wants to speak. At times he produces sounds which we find it difficult to identify as imitation; at others, he succeeds only in making ineffective silent gesticulations. When there is a real imitation of movement without speech, visual perception derives its exceptional motor efficiency from auditory memory. Thus, it is not the visual imitation of lip movements that leads to speech; rather, imitation of speech leads to imitation of lip movements.

Gutzmann (28) noted that when his second child was eight months old, he watched lip movements whenever he was spoken to. "I opened and closed my lips as I would to say *ba*, without making the sound. She imitated this movement without making the sound." [5] But we must remember that the child, at the age of eight months, already knew how to say *baba*; the author refers to this a little later on. There is therefore reason to believe that the imitation of the syllable observed by him had lent a motor quality to the sight of the silent articulation of *ba*.

The personal observations given above demonstrate the close connection that exists between a supposed imitation of movement and the effort to reproduce a sound — an effort that succeeds or fails depending on whether the sounds are well known or new, and whether the imitation is freer from or more dependent on the model.

Deaf-Mutes and Blind People. But one may object on the ground that imitation can lead to speech. This is the way a deaf-mute learns to read lips (or, to be more precise, to read faces), and even to talk.

In order to grasp the nature of this kind of learning, one must realize at the very outset that this learning process never occurs spontaneously. Only recently have people sought recourse to this type of learning; it is just as artificial as auditory learning is spontaneous. Besides, enormous difficulties are involved.

On the one hand, visual perception is insufficient to give any information about the complex movements of articulation. A good many sounds are made that entail no visible external ex-

5. Gutzmann, *Sprache und Sprachfehler*, p. 16.

pression such as movements of the lips or face. And so we must try other things: have the deaf-mute feel the breath as it escapes from one's mouth; make him *touch* one's throat, chest, nose, the top of one's head, so that he may perceive the particular vibrations that enable him to distinguish certain letters.

On the other hand, the deaf-mute must be taught to use this information as a *controlling* aid in learning to imitate. To be sure, many deaf-mutes can easily imitate visible movements of the body, legs, arms, or fingers. But some experts believe that training is necessary for vocal movements (51) (regulating the respiratory movements, breathing in by mouth and breathing out through the nose or vice versa; making a ball move on a grooved ruler by blowing on it continuously or in sharp spurts of breath; with the aid of the same procedure, rhythmically swinging a cork suspended from a string; blowing out a candle or making the flame waver; making little paper windmills re-volve; blowing up a bag or a balloon, etc.). In all these ingenious exercises we see a quest for control through touch or vision — in other words, through uniform perceptions of what the model and the imitator are doing. Certain experts (44) also suggest placing the pupil and the instructor in front of a mirror so that the pupil can compare the shape of the lip movements. We must add that this training generally does not begin before the child is six and that the exercises to overcome muteness include two years of schoolwork. Practically speaking, it is difficult to prevent the deaf-mute from abandoning language in favor of gestures and writing, even with those who live with him. The method is still the subject of controversy. Only an elite, with the aid of great perseverance, can practice lip reading properly or learn to speak.

Finally, in assessing the results, we must take into account the residual hearing of most deaf people. Today, efforts are concentrated mainly on making the most of this residual hear-ing, which hitherto had been neglected. Even a small amount of residual hearing may loom large in the success ascribed to the oral method. Inversely, we know that if a child becomes deaf before he is four years old, after having begun to talk, it is difficult to prevent him from completely losing the use of speech and becoming totally mute. We can see therefore, how insignificant a role compensation of hearing by vision plays here.

If all this is true, how can visual imitation in the education of the normal child, for whom learning to speak is a spontaneous kind of game, fulfill the role attributed to it?

To buttress the thesis of visual imitation, we have called attention to the fact that the first imitated sounds are the labial consonants (m, p). (However, the point made here is only half correct when presented in this way.) The dental consonants, which are not as accessible to vision because of the way they are enunciated, are noticeably contemporaneous. In addition, there are the guttural consonants, which are pronounced very early (k). Moreover, as we have seen, there is room for difference in interpretation.

It has also been said that an infant born blind is somewhat slow in learning to speak. This can be explained variously. Wundt, who cited this argument, also indicated that the blind child is hampered by the absence of perceptions that connect sound with its meaning (demonstrative gestures, the acts of the person who uses the word, etc.). Nonetheless, a blind child's handicap is *insignificant* in comparison with that of a deaf child. The blind never require artificial training in learning how to talk.

Thus, not only does the hypothesis that ascribes importance to vision encounter theoretical difficulties — since early imitation is scarcely intelligible and the data cited lend themselves to a variety of interpretations; it likewise cannot be reconciled with well-established facts. Thus the blind infant has no difficulty learning to talk whereas the deaf infant is condemned to total muteness, except those mute children who receive artificial training. But this is so complicated that training is not possible until the child reaches school age. Then training might belatedly give him an extremely imperfect substitute for speech. We will return to this when we discuss the general problem of visual imitation.

THE IMITATION
OF
MOVEMENTS

1. THE THEORY OF INSTINCT

I

Definitions. Vocal imitation, a limited problem and the object of rather thorough investigation by child psychologists, has provided us with a certain amount of insight into the mechanism of imitation. This will be helpful in our discussion of the more general aspects of the question. But because the terms used in dealing with this problem are extremely complex, we must first clearly define the imitation of acts.

1. Viewed externally, imitation may be said to exist when two similar beings perform the same act.

2. In order to be more precise, we must take the psychological circumstances into account. Perception or memory of the model's act will determine the actual performance as well as the nature of the imitator's act.

These two statements must be broken down as follows:

a) Sometimes imitation merely plays the role of stimulating agent. The act is familiar to the person who executes it. Here we are not comparing imitated acts with instinctive or habitual acts. In our terminology, any manifestation, whether acquired or innate, whose actual performance is suggested by the similar acts of others constitutes imitation. Our social life is typified first of all by the fact that natural modes of being or behaving, whether innate or individually acquired, are contagious; and their manifestation, even if spontaneous, is usually dependent on examples set by other members of society.

b) In other instances, imitation plays an educative, constructive role. Influenced by example, the child acquires a new type of act which he probably would never have achieved on his own. In this sense, imitation appears either as an aspect of the assimilation of traditions that perpetuate the modes of being or behaving characteristic of a given society or as an aspect of the generalization of an individual's innovative acts.

In the first instance, *a*, the similarity of the acts is directly due to the similarity of those who execute them; they possess an identical physical structure and an identical nervous system. Such similarity exists even among individuals who are removed from all influence by example.

In the second instance, *b*, similarity is sought and achieved through a learning process that involves trial and error and corrects initial attempts in order to attain an increasingly satisfying level of conformity. This conformity will vary according to the environment; it is not preformed in the species.

Between the two categories there are a whole series of intermediate stages. The second category represents a modification of the first: the new is grafted onto the old, custom onto instinct. Thus, laughter and tears are at once human reflexes and, in certain specific guises, conventional, ritualistic manifestations, determined by the social environment.

The term "similarity of acts" can mean many different things.

The act can be viewed in terms of its purpose, function, effects, and relation to an object; or it can be thought of as something physical, as an ensemble of movements.[1] The concept of similarity can be applied to either or both of these aspects. And identical results can be reached by different means, different movements. Inversely, an exact copy of movements can fail to produce in the imitator the effects his model strove to achieve and which gave to the model's gestures their raison d'être.

But this is not all. A complex act can be envisaged either in

1. Morgan [46a] suggested for these two different categories, the terms "copy" and "imitation," but they never became part of the commonly used vocabulary.

its totality or in one or another of its aspects. Often the agent is also the model. He himself is, in one part of his body, the object of an act executed by another part. Imitation may yield only one of these aspects, or it may express both. A child watches me polish my shoes. He may imitate me by brushing *my* shoes or by brushing *his*. In the first instance, he is imitating my gesture but behaves toward my foot as he would toward an *object*. In the second, not only is the gesture imitated, but the child relates it to a homologous part of his own body. It is thus evident that the intellectual meanings as well as the focuses of attention differ in the two instances. A person capable of the first act may be incapable of the second.

3. And now let us go further in our study of the mental state of the imitator. He can be *conscious* or *unconscious* of the fact that he is imitating. He may pay no attention to the objective similarity of acts; or, inversely, he may become more and more identified with his model. The phenomenon of subjective assimilation should become clear as a consequence of the preceding distinctions. One can be aware of the similarity of the results and yet remain unaware of the similarity of the elementary movements. One can be aware of the similarity between active gestures and yet not extend subjective assimilation to the whole person; or else one can do the opposite.

These definitions are necessary in order to avoid the misunderstandings and ambiguities to which many authors have fallen prey.

II

The Theory of a General Instinct for Imitation. The phrase "instinct for imitation" is often used. Usually it is not defined. However, we must make the effort if we wish to achieve something more than a literal explanation. Common sense seems to regard as acceptable the idea of an instinct to imitate — in its broadest sense but not in its narrow sense. There seems to be no particular difficulty in believing that the sight of an act performed by an individual of the same species will determine a similar act. Even the imitator's identification with his model, which this fact seems to imply, awakens no misgivings. Awareness of one's species, a kind of Platonic reminiscence, immediately is interpreted as imitation and a feeling of affinity. Apparently no need is felt to seek more subtle reasons.

One's mind moves so easily from the idea of *spontaneous* or *automatic* imitation to that of instinctive imitation that the latter probably benefits, in the minds of many, from all the data bearing on the former. We find, in certain kinds of descriptions, data about suggestion, about hypnotism, and about mental contagion, terms that support this hypothesis and even impose it. Psychologists and sociologists have generalized about them. Compayré (41) expressed a very widespread view when he wrote: "A kind of natural hypnotism irresistibly suggests imitative movements. The power of example communicates itself and spreads; it attracts and seduces the mature man and *with even greater reason* the child. . . . Such imitation cannot be effective unless it encounters in the individual thus prodded to action a natural tendency to accept and yield to the influence of example. And it is this tendency that constitutes in its initial form the instinct of imitation, a passive instinct, to be sure, that is really nothing more than the tendency to welcome the suggestions of others."

A well-known explanation of sympathy and esthetic emotion also derives from this view. According to Lipps (41), our natural instinct leads us to imitate gestures and facial expressions — that is, if no other influence intervenes to inhibit this tendency. Our attitudes tend to pattern themselves after those of others and to create moral inclinations which these attitudes express. This is the theory of *Einfühlung*. To be sure, Lipps stresses the point that an "internal" imitation is usually involved here. But what does this mean? It must signify an imitation that has been arrested in the very process of materialization by some mental complication; hence it presupposes a primitive and real imitation.

The primitive nature of imitation has been generally emphasized in recent works. A study by Finnbogason (25) demonstrates how far the systematic elaboration of this view can take us. Finnbogason admits that attentive perception, absorption in the spectacle of other people's activities, leads directly to imitation, that it is a necessary and sufficient precondition of the process of imitation. To be sure, he has made no special study of the child and does not explicitly advance the theory of instinct; but he inclines toward it. He can scarcely do otherwise, rejecting as he does the thesis that interposes the kinesthetic image of our own movements between perception of the model and imitation. More than that, he holds that imitation is quite a different thing from suggestion. If I smile when I see someone else smile, either I do so in a way that is natural to me, or else my smile is patterned after the smile of others. In the first instance, my smile is due to suggestion; in the second, it is the result of true imitation. Furthermore, the second kind of smile will occur whenever we are completely immersed in our own impressions. "Variations in the vital manifestations of our fellowmen are transmitted to us; they infect us, one may say, as soon as we become involved in observing them." This kind of imitation, which is related to whatever it is that may be unique in the model, is inspired not only by the example of other human beings but also by any sort of material form. Not only does the hand follow the contour of an object, the mimetic and plastic attitudes of the entire body delineate the form.

The Theory of Special Imitative Instincts. We see here the kind of generalizations put forward when the theory of imitation is regarded as a primitive phenomenon. But when viewed differently, the theory, on the contrary, becomes more limited and more precise. Forms of imitation hitherto looked upon as primitive can then be identified as *a collection of specific instincts.*

There is a priori nothing outlandish in the notion that a particular reaction might derive a sufficient stimulus from the perception of the same reaction in a member of the same species. This doubtless is not beyond the capacity of the inborn nervous system. But first two conditions must be met: the example must have motor efficiency, and the reaction must assume a specific form. If the special properties of a chemical stimulant, or the localization of a mechanical contact, produces a totally determinate response in an animal, why should the same not be true of the visual perception of a form in motion? And why should not this reaction be similar to the reaction that stimulates it? This similarity is in itself a secondary effect. Whether the subject is conscious of it is of no importance. The resemblance is not a precondition of the act; the latter springs from the distinctive structure of the neuromuscular system.

We have sufficient data to establish that certain complex visual perceptions may possess a special efficiency because of the presence of a preformed system. Rigidly fixed relations between certain species (predation, parasitism, commensalism) seem to be dictated by an instinctive visual recognition, at least for animals whose sense of vision is dominant. The same is perhaps also true for animals belonging to the same species, whose recognition of one another manifests itself in sexual, parental, and gregarious instincts. In the human species it is to these instincts that one is tempted to look in seeking confirmation of these views.

Accordingly, the idea of instinctive imitation becomes plausible. Such generic recognition — which, from a physiological point of view, is merely a special way of behaving — may include a particular category of reactions whose hallmark is resemblance to the reactions that stimulate them. One can explain in this way a good many facts about the life of the social animal. One can resolve the enigma of those disciplined movements which do not seem to be conditioned by hierarchy and language. Starting from this principle, one might try to draw up a list of instinctive imitations in man himself. It is true, of course, that child psychologists do not agree about how to enlarge the list. They seem to hesitate over a good many particular cases. Except for vocal imitation, the examples most frequently cited by Preyer (54), Stern (69), MacDougall (43), etc., relate to the contagious effect of certain manifestations of emotion — laughter, smiles, tears — or to such things as yawning, pouting, sticking out one's tongue, closing one's eyes, etc. The reason for this is that such forms of behavior appear at a very early age or cannot be explained by associations based on individual experience because of the heterogeneity in both subject and model of the mental images of these acts.

III

Instinct and Automatism. What then are we to think of the theories of instinct? In our discussion of speech we noted how difficult it is to analyze them. Let us begin by eliminating the most questionable arguments.

At the outset we must stress the importance of making a clear distinction between instinctive imitation and automatic imitation, whether in the normal or the pathological state. The origins of automatism are instinct and habit, and each is very different from the other. All the data borrowed from the life of the adult or the adolescent are inappropriate for establishing this distinction. Man imitates either deliberately or automatically depending upon the complexity of his mental state at the moment, but he is always capable of imitating. And we have every reason to believe that this aptitude is definitely acquired at the end of the second or third year. From very accurate observation of the fact that will power tends to inhibit automatism, one should not infer that automatism itself is not acquired. The descriptions given above therefore remain valid even though one has no a priori basis for applying them to the young child.

Moreover, the examples of automatic imitation assembled in the works of Finnbogason (25) and of Vigouroux and Juquelier (74) cannot all be interpreted in the same way. Contemporary psychiatry no longer views the phenomenon of suggestion, for example, as quite so simple as was once thought. Although it is not to be confused with deliberate acts, it is equally complex. In studies of hysteria, the psychic relations established between the experimenter and his subject are stressed. Ideas on training and on instinct are very far apart. The imbecile, as Dumas has demonstrated (23), may believe that he is being asked to imitate, and he may proceed to behave in a certain way either out of deference or in jest. Finally, we must repeat, the components of acts which the individual has long *known* how to perform stem from habits which are the prerequisites of suggestion through example.

Imitations and Reactions. One must also make a distinction between imitation of attitudes and gestures and imitation of vague movements or even static forms. Finnbogason submits that the attentive contemplation of a letter, for example the letter *D*, tends directly to produce movements or gestures expressive of its particular peculiarities. This may be true of the educated adult who knows how to write or draw; it is certainly not true of the small child. Delacroix (20) is quite correct when he says that perception persists in the imitative movements of the object and that this renders possible an analysis of the object. Such observations are valuable for a proper understanding of esthetic perception. But a goodly number of movements, and precisely those that most closely resemble imitation, are acquired. They constitute a part of the habits of an adult and are not genuinely instinctive reactions (like the use of one's hands to describe the shape or size of an object). The very slowness with which one learns to write or draw is highly significant. As Luquet (42) has shown, the child is slow to realize that it is possible to copy a given object, and, as we shall see, descriptive gestures occur considerably later than other forms of imitation. We concede that attentive, absorbed, fascinated perception is the most important prerequisite of imitation. But we still need to know whether it serves from the outset as the direct cause of faithful imitation, or whether at first it is merely a stimulus and a way of controlling experiments; and last, whether such control is direct or indirect.

The word imitation is equivocal when applied to all of the data we have been discussing. Does the subject react to the example itself or, because of earlier experiences, to a particular meaning that has been acquired by this example? Much of the data offered by Finnbogason as pertaining to imitation, in the sense of copying whatever is individual in the original act, consists instead in examples of mere suggestion of habitual acts. In the beginning, when the child responds to an individual, he is in no way emulating that person's special way of smiling or laughing. Later, however, he will try to conform to individual mannerisms. He will pattern some of his expressions after those of the people around him. This is not something inborn but rather the consequence of learning.

A good many of the instances mentioned in the preceding pages are not even pseudoimitations. As Darwin, here following Montaigne, has remarked, we feel like coughing when we listen to a speaker who has a cold. But do we try to mimic his particular, idiosyncratic cough? Not at all. We cough even if the speaker does not actually do so but is merely hoarse, as if we wished to clear our throat. In other words, we *react* to the perception of these sounds by recourse to habitual means, to avoid reproducing the same sounds ourselves. Similarly, according to an earlier observation made by A. Smith, spectators "imitate" the movements of a tightrope dancer; they react as if they themselves are involved, and move as if to correct a fall rather than copy it, just as we throw our body backwards when we see someone leaning over a precipice. The same is true when we "imitate" the movements of a man walking on ice who tries to regain his balance as he slips; or the efforts of someone trying to lift a heavy object; or the rhythmic cadence of marching troops, etc. Suggestion in the sense in which we are using it stems not only from the movements of the individual but also from the overall situation in which objective elements play not the slightest role. Still other imaginary objects intervene. These, not until now mentioned by me, probably appear only for a while, but they do lend additional significance to the examples already cited (the blow to be parried, the missile or vehicle to be avoided, etc.). The art of mimicry itself may owe some of its effectiveness to this kind of suggestion; and suggestion, in turn, is not a primitive phenomenon.

Genuine Instinctive Reactions. Many writers have also objected to the idea of a general instinct of imitation. MacDougall rejects it because he cannot reconcile it to the customary definition of instinct. The impulse to imitate lacks specificity both in its motor manifestations and in its emotional content. Its existence in animals is doubtful. Finally, most of the data that we have about it can be explained on some other basis. We will return to these arguments later. Criticism of the theory of instinct will become more exact when we succeed in making alternative explanations credible.

Let us now turn to the more precise forms of the theory. It is possible, by limiting the scope one ascribes to instinct, to avoid certain criticisms. Prandlt (53) wonders why the infant imitates the acts of a person but not the movement or form of a curtain. Schneider for his part remarks that the child ought to imitate the oscillation of a shiny ball instead of reaching out his hand for it. In answering both men, one can point out that only in *certain cases* do preformed sensory connections exist which make imitation possible. These reservations, however, demonstrate that only the negative nature of this theory shields it from criticism. One might demand that the champions of this theory should furnish precise data about the mechanism to which it alludes, or at least render such data more understandable by suggesting analogies with better-known facts.

Which sensory-motor systems in the young child are unquestionably preformed? Let us confine ourselves to those that, although responding to internal stimuli, are nonetheless regulated by visual sensations. The appearance or displacement of an object in the field of vision directs the *movements of the eyes and the head.* This enables the infant to follow the object with his eyes. I have observed this in the clearest possible manner on the fifth day (slow movement of the hand back and forth twenty-five centimeters from the infant's face, in front of a well-lit window). *Prehension* seems largely preformed in the sense that the infant's hand, which he does not see, is thrust in the direction where an object attracts his attention; perhaps movement in depth is by this time wholly regulated by visual perceptions (third and fourth month). The same is true of movements of *the head and part of the upper body* as the infant leans toward the fixed object (as early as the eleventh day). *Locomotion* is usually regulated from the very beginning by visual perceptions as well as by tactile and kinesthetic indications. The very early appearance of this mechanism is concealed because of the delay in muscular development. The legs, by being extended, participate (eleventh day) in the forward thrust of the body toward the object perceived. As early as the thirty-fourth day, the infant, held under his arms, executes complete walking movements (the feet are raised very high, the toes are stretched and flexed, depending on whether the foot is brought forward or made to rest on the ground) (L, 34th day and 37th day; P, 35th day). During this initial attempt to walk, the infant stares at the person who is calling to him. I noted the beginning of a movement *to climb* at an age (3:8) when the child had never seen this done. Even had he seen it, the imitation would still be surprising. Held under his arms (he did not yet walk unaided), he looked at an object above him that he wanted to reach. He raised his foot (which he could not see) several times as if seeking a perch. When offered one, he put his foot on it without looking and lifted the other foot. The knee was flexed and then stretched; these movements were determined instinctively by perception of an object too high to be reached with the hand.

In the same way, an infant carried in one's arms leans over by *bending his body forward* to reach an object placed so low that it is not within the reach of his hands (3:4). If, by holding the infant's hand, you prevent him from bringing it to his mouth, he looks at the hands thus immbolized, then *lowers his head* toward it (L, 3:4). As soon as L was able to take a few steps on her own (11:10), she *stooped* in an effort to pick up a marble lying on the floor. But being too far away from it, she stood up, took the necessary two additional steps and again stooped to pick up the marble that was now exactly within her reach. Certain movements which we might assume to be imitated are on the contrary essentially spontaneous, since they differ greatly from the movements that an adult or a much older child would be capable of executing. For example, when we get up from our hands and knees, we shift our weight to one knee in order to free the other. Then we bend our leg and place the foot flat on the ground in order to stand up. A child of one or two never does this. He extends both legs simultaneously, moves his feet closer to his hands, which have remained stationary, then *stands up* by straightening up on both legs. Nor do I believe that the child owes to example the way he chooses his movements. Climbing over a barrier, getting down from a high piece of furniture, etc., are among the activities that the child learns with a minimum of trial and error. They seem to be directly controlled by vision.

Each of the activities alluded to so far is, however, a simple reaction, a movement of the limbs or body in space as determined by the visible properties of solid bodies in general. The entire mechanism has to do with the most general conditions of the life of relationships, with the relations between the living being, endowed with movement, and the *material environment in general*. Not at all involved are the special relationships that unite the living being with individuals of the same species and with members of his own social group. However, the theory of instinct represents these special relationships as being subordinated to visual sensation through hereditary automatism.

The Belated Nature of Imitation. Whereas the reactions we have described grow more and more precise as a consequence of practice, the first six or seven months of life are marked in their entirety, as Baldwin (1) has observed, by the *absence of imitation*. The infant does not imitate, despite all our efforts to encourage him. He remains a mere spectator of all the activities that arouse his interest and which he would plainly like to see repeated. His psychic excitation is manifested by cries, smiles, and laughter. The infant's eyes follow the individual or the object. He reaches out toward it, waves his arms, moves his legs. After the fourth month he even seizes objects and shakes them, or puts them in his mouth. But he does not imitate the acts offered him as models. For a long time he will bang forks, knives, and spoons on the table (L, end of the sixth month), although he has never seen anyone else do this. At this stage, any premature efforts to get the child to imitate the simplest acts are doomed to failure. If one tries to use the infant's toys (dolls, stuffed animals) to stimulate an appropriate act, he merely bangs them or puts them in his mouth. At this age the infant is interested in watching other children play; but he does not participate except in the most casual manner. L (six months) would burst out laughing when her older brother made a funny face. But she made no attempt to imitate him then, although later she invariably tried to do so.

If one eliminates from so-called instinctive imitation everything that can be explained by the influence of the same general circumstances on the two children, or everything that is due to the influence of associational transfer phenomena, then the entire domain becomes so narrow that one is tempted to agree with Ferretti when he concludes (24): "In short, all that remains of heteroimitation that is uniquely due to special instincts is perhaps the act of protruding one's lips or sticking out one's tongue. Would it be overly subtle to suggest that, among the few children who reacted in this way, some connections due to personal experience might have been established between the kinesthetic sensations of the mouth and the visual presence of other mouths (for example, the way lips are protruded in the act of kissing)?" Later, I will present other hypotheses of this kind and buttress them with a few observations.

The Relationships of Instinct and Imitation. Since for activity in general, as well as for vocal utterances, true instinctive reactions do not constitute imitation, there is good reason to examine the genesis of imitation. That is, we must connect it with the primitive reactions from which it springs as a consequence of being subordinate to new perceptions — a process that is influenced by the physical and social environment.

One simple example borrowed from animal psychology will suffice to clarify the method.

The baby chick seems to be led to peck because of the mother hen's attitude: an apparent invitation to her young to imitate by example. But actually, if we press the point of a pencil into the ground, or drop small objects from a tweezer, the chick will be stimulated to peck. The stimulus therefore operates in spite of the fact that the chick sees no being similar in appearance to the members of its own species executing a movement likely to invite imitation. Moreover, the perception that stimulates this innate reflex is to be found precisely within the experience of most chickens. This experience is associated with the visual perception of the specific being (the chicken), making a specific movement of the head and neck (pecking). These associations are incidental to the hereditary nervous organization of the chicken. They are not incidental to the ordinary, normal conditions of the chicken's development.

All instincts, especially those related to imitation in man, probably operate in this way. The child responds to the perception of the adult and his action; the play of inherited mechanisms is implicit in his responses. But one cannot say a priori which of the elements of a complex perception are involved. Probably not all of them are until the experience of their interdependence endows them with this power. The first manifestation of the instinct does not affect all the circuits which will in the end unite every detail of the perception with every detail of the response. Who can identify with any certainty the sensitive elements with which the inherent tendencies of the sexual, parental, or social instincts are linked? This is an immense field and one that has scarcely been explored scientifically, despite all the assumptions we tend to make about the present state of our knowledge. Perhaps one day the roots of what we incorrectly call instinctive imitation will be uncovered.

Instincts and Predisposition. There is a further difficulty. Because of the arbitrary way in which I defined instinct in the first part of this book, I may be accused of brushing aside the phenomenon of instinctive imitation. In addition to the innate responses that are truly independent of any learning process — I have cited examples of this in the foregoing pages — we should perhaps include hereditary traits. These, although not powerful enough to enable stimuli to determine acts, nonetheless make subsequent learning easier without rendering it altogether unnecessary. Infinitely greater flexibility in hereditary patterns appears to be a possibility. We may even go as far as to argue that no part of the ancestral experience will then be lost. But to make this seductive theory scientifically valid, we must have an exploratory method; and as yet we do not have one. To be sure, recent studies on the training of several generations of animals, conducted according to the method of economy in recurrences, have yielded some good results. But we can only compare and contrast individuals who are not subject to the operation of the same hereditary factors. Such a method does not enable us to examine, in the human species, the instinctual root of social habits, and of imitation in particular.

In summary, then, theories pertaining to instinct tend to waver between two tendencies. The thrust of one tendency is to limit the application of ideas to facts that are well established and independent of the learning process. There is some danger that it may lead to an oversimplification of complex data, and it can therefore be criticized for want of subtlety and nuance. The other tendency ascribes to instinctive factors a role in all the phenomena of psychic life. This is probably correct, but there is an ever present risk of failing to pinpoint the data and of continuously confusing the inherited with the acquired, the physiological with the social factors. The first tendency seems preferable to me for methodological reasons and also because it is conducive to greater clarity. In studying the learning process that leads to imitation, we are certain to be examining the elements of a genuine history, since this process is a necessary precondition despite the facility and shortcuts that may result from innate predispositions. Short of employing a method that involves residual attributes which cannot be otherwise explained, it is impossible to uncover the phenomenon of instinct without introducing some measure of ambiguity.

2. SELF-IMITATION AND IMITATION OF OTHERS

I

Self-Imitation. Of all the changes that affect a child's organism, only a few attract his attention and stimulate his activity. Sensations of pain alone are capable of arousing sustained reactions. They constitute a closed cycle in the sense that they reach a culmination only when the pain disappears, unless exhaustion or some other very powerful diversion intervenes. Thereupon, the interrupted equilibrium is reestablished — and it can be reestablished in no other way. Through the duration of these reactions, regardless of how varied they may be, it is the sensation of pain that gives unity to the mental state and limits it in time.

The same characteristic phenomena recur when "interesting" sensations are felt, at least for as long as they remain interesting. If the factors that produce these phenomena are unable to sustain them for any length of time, reactions occur which reach their culmination only when the sensation itself reappears (unless fatigue or some other diversion intervenes). Here again, the entire course of the phenomenon is determined by a definite impression; the child "seeks out" the sensation he has just experienced. In the beginning it does not matter that the sensation is the result of his own movements, or the more or less direct consequence of something he has experienced — for example, some physical attention that has been bestowed upon him, or some event that he has witnessed. The reproduction of the interesting sensation may result directly from the infant's reactions; or it may occur accidentally, and somewhat later, with or without the intervention of another person. Occasionally the infant's efforts will prove unsuccessful or his desire will remain unfulfilled. But repetition of certain identical experiences will make possible a choice of efficient modes of activity. Self-imitation or circular reaction will therefore occupy an increasingly important place in the psychic life of the infant.

Here it will be well to adduce a few typical developments that occur at an early age. From the very first day one notes that when the breast is removed from the mouth of a nursing baby, he seeks it again in oscillating lateral movements. L (0:15) put her hand in her mouth and tried, unsuccessfully the first time, to put it back after it had been removed. She held on to the pencil that had been put in her hand and squeezed it tightly when we tried to take it away. By her attitude she seemed to be asking us to continue to dance with her. When the movements stopped, she began to cry; when they recommenced, she subsided.

Later, the objects her hands touched served to determine indefinitely similar faltering movements she made as she endeavored to grasp and scratch. For more than fifteen minutes she gripped fistfuls of the material on a cushion (2:15); she played with her dress for a long time, thumb opposed, never glancing at her hand as she did so. The quest for tactile and kinesthetic sensations is likewise evidenced in caresses (scratching herself and being scratched by someone; rubbing her cheeks or nose against the face of the person holding her) and in the exploration of parts of her own body or someone else's (knee, foot, hair, beard, clothes).

For half an hour she amused herself by shaking a little bell, or else made clumsy attempts to push down the keys of the piano (4:8). In these instances, the effects of auditory sensation were combined with those of tactile and kinesthetic sensations.

Visual sensations were also in evidence: watching or recovering a moving object (0:29), or finding a person who is no longer in the same place (2:5); watching one's hand as it opens and shuts (4 months).

Simplified hiding games also demonstrate the tendency to provoke — indirectly this time — the repetition of an interesting sensation (a person appears and then disappears behind a curtain). When L was five months old her role was passive, but by the time she was eight months old she began to take an active part in playing. The following game gave her a great deal of pleasure: her brother would lunge toward her as if to grab her, and the person holding her would quickly move her away to elude him.

The prehensile movements that occurred after the fifth month led to interminable games with a chain, a ring, a medal, a rattle. At six months L liked to bang on the table endlessly with any solid objects she could hold. She would fly into a temper when she dropped them.

There is no need to cite further examples. Our purpose is to point out how early in the life of an infant these well-known types of reactions occur. Preyer has frequently been quoted for having noted that his son opened and closed the lid of a box seventy-nine times in a row, after he had accidentally discovered how to do it. The patience with which infants endlessly, tirelessly repeat the same movements, the same words, is well known; it is a *psychological characteristic* of infancy.

But in studying the circular reaction, writers usually confine their attention to pleasurable sensations. I feel it is preferable to investigate *interesting* or *unusual* ones. In exceptional cases, disagreeable or painful sensations can provoke this circular reaction, at least until sensations of the opposite kind intervene to reverse the process.

The following observations were recorded at the end of P's first year and the beginning of the second.

P pricked himself with a pin or with the point of a paper knife and tried to reproduce this sensation by uttering a sharp cry each time (12 months).

His finger having been pinched in a door (or later in the top of a washing machine), he tried to put his finger back in the same spot (12:23).

Having pushed his finger into a keyhole, he cried because he could not pull it out without assistance. But he immediately recommenced this dangerous experiment. (14:15).

He burned his finger a little by removing a small piece of red-hot charcoal from the fireplace. He soon tried to do it again, but this time he was far more cautious, etc. (12:13).

The Mechanism of Self-Imitation. Circular reaction is therefore a very general phenomenon. How does one explain its mechanism?

In certain cases the efficient response is immediate. It occurs almost without trial and error. The excitation is immediately channeled toward those faculties that insure its continuity or repetition. The shift on the retina of a mobile object which is watched closely by the infant produces a reflex rotary motion of the eye and head by which the central perception is preserved or reestablished.[2] But should the object move outside of the field of vision, the infant will seek it by trial and error. This break in the equilibrium no longer results in an automatic correction but rather in oscillations of the eyes and the head, even in movements of the entire body. In some cases there are signs of emotional upset (impatience, disappointment) that will be expressed by general efforts, by cries, or tears. The disappearance of an interesting perception produces *trials* in sensory, motor, or other adaptations whose efficient results, if there are any,

2. The difference, however, between such a reaction and the one that follows it is not very great. This is proved by the flexibility of visual adaptation (elasticity of the convergence within certain limits; variety of movements that correspond to the same shift of the image on the retina, Marina's experiment, etc.) Cf. Koffka (35).

will become the objects of subsequent selections. Such "trials" will be associated with certain details of the situation (for example, seeking a heavy object on the floor, or an inert object concealed in someone's hands, etc.).

Reactions of the first type may be regarded as specific instincts of one kind or another (adaptive reflexes of the senses, touch, posture, etc.). Reactions of the second type — in which certain elements of the first type are present — develop into habits that are, however, modified by experience and selection.

Just as one progresses unconsciously from instinct to habit, so there is a gradual transition from the immediate effect of the sensation to the effect of the latent memory, and from latent memory to the image itself. When the object moves within the field of vision, the sensations themselves are the controlling factors; when it moves out of the field of vision, the memory is called into play. In some cases this memory is precise and tenacious. P (3:9), sitting on his bed, followed me with his eyes. When he lost sight of me, he would persistently look for me for a while, not allowing himself to be fooled by others who tried to distract him. The unity of the psychic state and the hazards of selection depend upon the persistence of the memory.

We must emphasize this essential idea. The affective value of the result does not necessarily correspond to a mastery of the appropriate means for achieving it.

Motor impotence is a characteristic feature of early infancy. Continuation or repetition usually depends on the cooperation of other people. The infant demands it by his attitude long before he can act on his own. In other words, he reacts with emotions of joy or disappointment according to whether his expectation is thwarted or gratified. The people who take care of the infant are often reduced to trial and error in finding out what he wants. As a consequence, the development of the means by which the infant seeks the help of others will tend to be synchronized with the growth of his own motor activity. Attitudes, emotional expressions, and finally language are among the elements involved in the process. "Again!" is one of the first words in an infant's vocabulary. It is used especially to obtain, through the help of others, an effect that is pleasing to him and which he is incapable of producing himself.

Be that as it may, interesting perceptions invariably eventually acquire, if they do not already possess it as the very outset, enough motor efficiency to insure their recurrence. Some of these perceptions consist of effects achieved only with the aid of others (this is the important function of language); others result solely from individual efforts coupled with the requisite, appropriate movements. This learning process is of major importance in developing the capacity to imitate others. Bain shows that progress in this type of imitation depends mainly on the extent of the child's spontaneous activity. Baldwin (1, 2) stresses this point in all his writings. Ferretti (24) notes that "there is a gradual transition from the immediate repetition of one's own movements to the repetition of a movement actually produced by someone else." He correctly emphasizes the fact that in both instances there is something similar about the infant's interest in imitation. The desire for imitation is not automatic; rather, imitation is sought for its affective quality. In the course of trial and error, certain objects, certain visible results, come to suggest specific actions. As the objective elements in the perception of other people's acts are discovered, they will, by communicating a motor quality to the example, become the source of future imitations.

II

The Knowledge of One's Own Body. In any effort to achieve true imitation, the act to be executed must be influenced by the model's similar act. But a special difficulty arises in this connection. Sensations of any kind that are or become regulators of the infant's spontaneous acts very frequently differ from the sensations whereby the infant recognizes the similar acts of others. Generally speaking, what happens here is quite different from the perception of voices. The sound the infant becomes aware of is an objective, clearly homogeneous element, regardless of whether it emanates from the person speaking or from the person imitating the speaker. Self-imitation naturally paves the way for imitation of others. Acts, on the contrary, involve primarily visual perception when they pertain to the acts of others, whereas the visual element is altogether secondary when applied to oneself.

The infant does not directly see all the parts of his own body. Some he rarely sees at any time; if he does see them, he usually perceives only one particular aspect. Some parts of his body may come into his field of vision without his even noticing them.

It is easy to trace the limits of this visual knowledge. Passive movements of the limbs may already have attracted the infant's attention. For example: I would put P's hand or foot on the piano and press down the keys (3:14) so he could "play" the piano. Similarly, when trying at the end of the fourth month to reach objects he would raise his right hand to eye level and keep moving it first closer to his eyes, then farther away from them. At this stage, he would stare at his hand when we cut his fingernails; he would put his hand right in front of his eyes and wiggle his fingers (3:23). In prehensile movements controlled by sight (from 3:17 on), the infant's attention is naturally drawn to his hand as he makes fumbling attempts to seize an object or handle it after he has done so. A little later (4:7 to 4:12), P became interested in movements of his feet and toes. He grabbed hold of his foot (5:2) and put it in his mouth.

My records show that L behaved in the same way. She would amuse herself by watching the movements of her hand in front of her eyes (2:23 to 3:3); she would grasp her knee and try to reach her foot, whose movements she observed with curiosity (3:27).

In short, visual attention is focused on the limbs and above all on their mobile extremities (hands, feet).

Other parts of the body are far less familiar to the infant. The chest and abdomen are seen only partially and then under special conditions. Some parts of the body attract the infant's attention because of certain acquired habits (for example, P became aware of his navel because of a game we used to play with him: we would press his navel as if it were a doorbell, imitating the noise of a bell); or because of the importance of their functions (urinary organs). But usually the infant looks at his body when it is clothed, and even then he sees it partially and incompletely. His back, head, and face are not subject to his direct visual perception.

We shall designate as *objects* those parts of the body that the infant knows by sight. At first, the infant apparently has no difficulty imitating acts that interest him. The visual image of moving hands and feet probably acquires a motor function that results from the mechanism of self-imitation. Motivated by some kind of accidental excitation, the infant may make a visible movement which he seeks to reproduce, fumbling and trying again until he succeeds. He is then able to see what he has done. This may explain a remarkably precocious feat performed by L. She imitated, by a rotary movement of the wrists, the dance of puppets. She watched my hands very attentively and began to make a few very indecisive movements herself. From time to time she looked at her own hands and moved them, as if she were comparing my movements to hers (4:22). Two days later, she did this again. She was lying in her crib, flat on her back with arms along her sides. She rotated her wrists, but her fingers were spread out and her forearms were not bent. Forgotten for a while, this game was repeated during the seventh month, either when we initiated it by setting the example or in response to the song that accompanied the puppet dance. One day, when she was imitating this movement with one hand, I made the same movement with both my hands. She immediately imitated me, watching her hands as if to make the comparison.

The Difficulties of the Problem. But these explanations have only a limited significance. How can imitation be extended to those parts of the body that are not subject to visual perception?

In the following acts, there is probably something that may be regarded as part of a visual perception comparable to the perception of another person: bending over, kneeling, bending one's body backward or forward, nodding one's head, opening or closing one's eyes and mouth, sticking out one's tongue, frowning, touching one's nose or ear. The same may be said about facial expressions — a grimace, a smile, raising one's eyebrows, twisting one's mouth.

Even the movements of visible parts of the body involve invisible clues. For example, the infant sees me raise my arm to eye level or above my head; if he is to associate my movements with his own, the fact that he can confine these movements to homologous parts of the body is not enough. By using the term "homologous," I mean to indicate that he identifies his head with mine, his arm with mine, etc. He still must learn to realize that our movements are identical. Doesn't this presuppose a comparison of *images as a whole*? Let us say that the infant sees me read a letter. If he is to imitate me exactly, he will have to realize that the sheet of paper must be in the same position in relation to his eyes and body as it was in relation to mine. He could do it if, from a geometric point of view, he had two homogeneous and similar mental images of our positions; but in one position the parts of the body will have to intervene as elements, and he has not yet been able to achieve a direct visual perception of them.

This problem apparently has escaped many authors who have studied imitation. Baldwin (1), although he has thoroughly delineated the idea of self-imitation, does not raise this question when he accepts the easy and immediate transition from self-imitation to the imitation of others. "When the organism, as a consequence of cerebral development, becomes capable of new adaptations, it ceases to be satisfied with the *contemplation* of objective movements; it begins finally to *imitate* them. And, *naturally*, it imitates people." That an infant should be especially interested in people goes without saying; but that he *knows* how to imitate them is something that requires explana-

tion. The regulatory perceptions that intervene in self-imitation are generally very different from those that operate in the
contemplation of the objective movements of others. How can
the latter possess the special motor efficiency of the former?

Let us try to classify the hypotheses that may explain the
transition from one to the other. Such hypotheses can rest on
either of the following postulates: the infant's perception of his
own acts constitutes the point of departure for this transition;
or his perception of the acts of others serves as the point of
departure. According to the first hypothesis, a kind of general
innate correlation, or one established as a consequence of early
experience, will enable the infant to transform tactile and
kinesthetic data into visual images. The second hypothesis presupposes that he will transform visual data into tactile and
kinesthetic images and thus render apparent the similarity between the acts of the model and those of the imitator.

3. THEORIES OF ASSOCIATION

I

The Construction of the Visual Image of One's Own Body. Certain objects yield a twofold experience — visual and tactile —
that enables us to evoke the visual image when we touch a
familiar object without seeing it — in the dark, for instance.
This twofold experience may be so quickly generalized that
the same transformation will extend even to new objects; it is
as if we possess *general formulas for transforming the tactile
into the visual* instead of mere particular memories. The same
is true when my attention turns to a certain part of my body of
which I have had no visual experience. This part of my body
as well as the area it occupies will yield an imaginative, visual
construction that is more or less precise. I tend to visualize my
aching tooth, a foreign body in my mouth, and even my internal

organs whenever my attention is drawn to them because of some anomaly.

One may therefore conclude that the infant gradually constructs a visual image of his body and movements, even if he has never happened to contemplate them in a mirror. As this image becomes more specific, it will become assimilated with the objective perception of the human body of others. Imitation therefore will be founded on assimilation that will be only a specific instance of the development of the idea of space.

This is the thesis which the German psychologist Prandlt (53) advanced earlier in attempting to explain sympathy (*Einfühlung*). Unlike Lipps (41), whose explanation he criticizes, Prandlt does not believe that sympathy is based on instinctive imitation. Rather, having investigated the assimilation attributable to the experience of gestures, of self-expression and the expression of others, he claims that the common precondition of the latter is sympathy and imitation. He is keenly aware of the complexities of the problem. "I never have an optical perception of my face or my features save when I look in the mirror, whereas the faces and expressions of others strike me at first as being only a complex of lines and colors." What is the psychological intermediary between a purely kinesthetic perception of my face and the purely visual perception of other people's faces? It is a visual image of my own face, linked through resemblance to the visual image of other people's faces, and tied through contiguity to my tactile and kinesthetic sensations. This image is gradually formed and grows more precise in a very indirect way. Sensations similar to those experienced by the skin of the invisible parts of the body have been felt in the visible parts. They can therefore serve as the means of visualizing a colored surface. Rough as this image may be, it nonetheless forms the basis upon which the infant builds the visual image of his own face. An important contribution is later made by tactile perceptions that add certain data about the spatial characteristics of the face. By touching one's limbs it is possible to form a tactile image of them. This image may differ markedly from the visual image; nevertheless, the former tallies with the latter, thanks to the spatial extension of sensations. The infant is able to assess the shape and size of his leg regardless of whether he actually looks at it or merely touches it with his hand. What occurs, therefore, is a reciprocal association of tactile and visual perceptions. It therefore follows that if the tactile image of one part of my body (my face, for example) is available to me, its spatial qualities will serve as a canvas that I need only fill in with colors in order to obtain a visual image. The same mechanism unifies the color image by means of the association that has been effected, so far as the visible parts are concerned, between the color itself and the tactile properties.

In short, this theory, which favors certain mental constructs, says that the spatial portions known at first in a heterogeneous way in the end become united in a homogeneous image. This is true of our body's image as well as of the images of other objects. Moreover, our body is continuously entering into relationships with visible objects (we see the shape of our head on the pillow, etc.). All these images merge. Since I am able to imagine the relations of objects that are part of partial, non-simultaneous, visual perspectives, united solely because of my movements, why doesn't my body itself, with all its various positions and movements, likewise become a part of my visual picture? Why shouldn't I possess an image of my own self *as seen from the outside*?

Criticism. We can certainly say in answer to this theory that the existence of such an image is not completely beyond the realm of possibility. However, it is rarely experienced by man and is even less likely to occur in an infant.

People tend too often to examine the association between images and sensations in the abstract. Their reasoning is based on a general outline of the phenomenon which defines the evocation of the image according to the abstract preconditions of possibility, resemblance, and contiguity. Examples are usually drawn from human psychology and chosen from among disinterested constructs of an artificial nature rather than from the close web of utilitarian thought. We forget that there is a *normal meaning*, an associational function. When I touch an object and elicit certain exploratory movements, it is not the form, position, or movement of my body that preoccupies me, but rather the attributes of the object. If visual images appear, they relate to the *object*. To be sure, tactile and kinesthetic data are preconditions of the image, but such data directly evoke the visible form of the object, not the visible forms, positions, or movements of our limbs. Accustomed to regulating his behavior on the basis of his visual perceptions of the object, a man who must act without seeing, in the dark, for example, tends to *imagine*, on the basis of other actual sensations, *what he would see* if it were light. The image is merely a substitute for the impossible sensation. It intervenes, not because of the effect of a disinterested association, but as a consequence of its normal *function*, to the extent that the image supplements the defective regulatory sensation. But whereas the visual sensations that stem from objects fulfill this function normally, it is very rare, on the other hand, that we have to look at our limbs in order to make them move. The visual image in this instance is unnecessary, and even though it may exist, this is most unlikely.

But what happens when the body of the subject itself becomes the object of his attention? This question is in the case of movements that are not subordinate to external objects, or in tactile exploration of the body itself. Usually there is no visual image. When the hand is placed in the area where an abnormal sensation is felt, the movement is regulated by local sensations and by kinesthetic indications. We know that this image can be created, in some cases, for those parts of the body that are known through sight. Of course, the subject tends to *look* at the area involved and his reaction is thereafter determined by both sight and touch. If he does not look at the area, he can *imagine what he would see* if he did. Thus, the image functions as a substitute for the absent sensation. But, by the same token, it is altogether improbable that such an image will normally appear in the place of what is not usually seen. If it did, the subject's reactions would be regulated neither by visual perceptions nor by the corresponding images.

The visual image created under such circumstances corresponds to secondary and belated psychic needs rather than to the general regulation of movements. Even a cultivated adult rarely develops such a visual image. E. Milhaud, in his study of the external projection of visual images (*Rev. philos.* 1894, p. 216), shows that in the matter of the localization of the imagined object, the subject *feels* as if he is somehow transported to the vicinity of the objects he imagines. "Does he *see* himself as being close to these objects? Some people say that this never happens to them. Others, although they never see themselves spontaneously, manage to do so when they concentrate and try very hard. And last, still others see themselves in a definitely spontaneous manner." The author cites two examples taken from this last group. In one, the subject states that he *can* see himself *vaguely*; in the other, an individual sees himself as if he were being *introduced*. This somewhat unusual case arouses our interest because of the subject's feeling that he wants to assume a very proper attitude; we try to see ourselves because we wonder how others see and judge us.

The Formation of the Visual Image. From the foregoing we may conclude that this type of visual image is rather exceptional in nature. Since, however, it does occur occasionally, and since it can be produced in response to a concentrated effort, we must try to uncover the procedures that make its existence possible.[3]

In view of the heterogeneity of these two kinds of data, it would seem that a visual interpretation of the body's tactile and kinesthetic data will always imply a prior association through contiguity. This type of association occurs either because one's eyes shift in order to see, or because there is a shift

3. Unless we presume that it is not itself a *product* of imitation, which it actually is most of the time.

in the field of vision of the part of the body involved. But it is precisely our body, both in its entirety and in some of its parts, that is the *only* object that cannot be seen as a consequence of a shift of this kind. One must therefore seek recourse in more indirect procedures.

Let us try to produce certain complex tactile sensations in an individual and then ask him to give us a visual interpretation. For example, let us draw a letter on his skin, but in a part of the body that he cannot see at that particular moment or that he will never be able to see. Then let us ask him to read the letter to himself. The tests I have made on an eight-year-old confirm the results that classical experiments have yielded.

I give a child four symbols to look at: ⌊ ⌈ ⌋ ⌉. He is asked to point to the one he thinks has been drawn on his skin. To simplify matters, we limit the areas on which the test is made: first we select the forehead and face; then the back of the head and neck. The results are very clear, and they do not vary. When the back of the head and neck are chosen, the subject reads the symbols as does the observer who stands behind him. When the forehead and face are selected, the subject points to the mirror images of the symbols which the observer sees in front of him.

In the course of these experiments on an eight-year-old, one often observes a movement of the hand, which the subject, after a moment of hesitation, tends to place near the part of the body that has actually been touched. Guided by the persistence of the tactile impression, or by immediate recall, the subject's hand follows the contour of the letter and sometimes repeats the same movements before his own eyes afterward. We may presume that once these movements have actually been executed, they tend to be repeated only mentally. Finally, after a little practice, they cease to be necessary because the reading of the letter *has become* direct. We notice that the movement of the arm or finger as it follows the tracing of the letter is already almost visible. It becomes entirely so when the arm moves somewhat away from the face without in any way modifying the movement. The shift of the movement from the neck to the field of vision is a little more complicated. It is doubtless made easier by prior learning, by the exploration of familiar objects that actually can be brought into the field of vision.

This test, consisting as it does of the reading of a letter, may seem somewhat artificial. But what we want to know is whether a learning process similar to the one that goes on in such experiments likewise occurs under normal conditions. When the infant puts his hand to his head, he can see a part of his arm movements; at the same time he experiences a series of tactile and kinesthetic sensations. He is therefore already prepared to use this procedure in order to create the visual image, *which does not mean that this use precedes the need felt for it.*

In short, the visual image of the body and of its various positions is ultimately achieved in an altogether indirect way. Even then it remains fitful and elusive. It encompasses details rather than the whole; it yields the outlines and the direction rather than an overall view. Since this visual image is obtained by means of an analytical process, it cannot give a true picture of the whole save at the cost of an extremely laborious synthetic effort, which will never become spontaneous. Is it possible for the infant to identify himself with us by means of such images? And can these images subsequently serve to make his acts conform to the example set? This is all the more unlikely since it is the infant's "synthetic incapacity" that truly characterizes his imagination. In other words, he is incapable of making the connection between the particular and the general, the form, order, or proportion, and this deficiency is still very apparent later on when he attempts his first drawings (Luquet, 42). Conversely, the infant perceives similarities between general effects, but at first he does not analyze them. Therefore it is quite unlikely that the processes which we have just described will be able, before the close of the first year, to provide the infant with personal images that can serve as a basis for imitation.

To repeat: the visual image of one's own body is an exceptional phenomenon. When Prandlt writes: "I cannot consciously change a single facial feature without at the same time experiencing an image of the visible aspect of this change," he is either contradicting experience or else the word *conscious* as used here suggests that artificial introspection tends to create such an image. For to ask oneself whether one imagines oneself visually is to attempt to do so, something which, to a certain extent, is perhaps possible. But before accepting the notion that an infant can create such an image one must first be able to prove that the infant touches his face and limbs intentionally rather than accidentally, that he does so in fact in order to construct a geometrically contoured image. And above all one will have to prove that an impression of similarity will result from this effort. Prandlt himself has had to admit that the transference of similar colors to similar parts of the body cannot yield, from the tactile point of view, a colored image of lips, tongue, or eyes. Since it is in fact achieved by analysis, how can this geometrical pattern, this colorless mask, speak to an infant's imagination?

II

The Construction of the Tactile Image of Others through Geometric Touch. Let us now turn to our second hypothesis. Because of innate or rapidly acquired potentialities, the infant can transform the visual perception of the model and its movements into tactile or kinesthetic images. In this way he absorbs the personal data which presumably regulate his own movements. It has often been said that vision is a form of touching from a distance — that in seeing an object one can imagine the sensations which tactile exploration would yield. The sight of other people's bodies would therefore evoke images analogous to the sensations that the subject procures for himself when he touches his own body. In this way he would become aware of the resemblance.

We must repeat and emphasize our serious reservations about the first hypothesis regarding the reality of these evocative images under normal conditions. Usually the transformation of the visual into the tactile is of little significance. Motor properties are transferred from touch to sight. Sight governs reaction from the outset and once the habit has been established, it can dispense not only with preliminary touch but also with tactile memory, which leaves no trace in the consciousness of an infant. At the most, one may encounter in certain cases a slight mental anticipation of the next sensation which makes recognition and control possible.

But we must quickly add that even if we try to create these images, they will yield no solution to the problem. They merely epitomize the individual, seen as a form, like some vague object. Are we to presume that the infant compares these images to the ones he can obtain by tactile explorations of his body? And will these images reveal to him the similarity of forms, or, in the wake of even more complex analyses, the similarity of positions and movements? Actually, when an intelligent adult feels an unknown, intricately shaped object without seeing it, he can assess its geometric resemblance to a model that he sees but *does not touch.* And he may be able to perceive the similarity of their movements. Are we to believe that such a feat can be performed by a one-year-old? Are we even to presume that he can acquire, through tactile exploration, a precise notion of both the form of his own body and its movements?

The Construction of the Tactile Image of Others through Qualitative Touch. But there is another way to interpret the transformation of the visual into the tactile. Instead of considering the manual sensation — which in active touching is associated with the sensation of moving a limb, and is expressed by the notion of a definite form as the outside limit of exploratory movements — let us concentrate on the *quality* of the contact, which varies according to the part of the body touched. In the case of my own body, this quality is intimately associated with local sensations felt in the area itself. These sensations intervene directly in the regulation of my movements. Because of this association, touching certain parts of other people's bodies can give me a kind of *sympathetic perception* of another individual rather than the perception of a geometric form. And visual perception, which in turn is associated with tactile perception, will indirectly be able to suggest to me the profound as well as the superficial impressions that flow from the corresponding parts of my own body — in other words, the elements I must possess if imitation is to become feasible. It is not beyond the realm of possibility that such associations do play a part. For example, P (11:25) sees me lying down. My eyes are closed. He is urged to "sleep" like me. He hesitates, *touches* first his mother's eyes, then mine. Finally, he blinks his eyes but does not shut them completely. Possibly, the special quality of the sensation felt when he touched our eyes awakened the memory of an analogous sensation experienced when he put his hand on his own eyes, and this may have determined the reflex of closing his own eyelids. But if this explanation is valid, the infant will actually have had to explore the body of other people, which in fact he has done only in a very incomplete and exceptional way. In this instance, unlike the prior one, the general habit of transforming visible into tangible forms — a process applicable to the human body as some vague or new object — is not involved. The transition from what has not been perceived in others to what has only been felt in oneself rests upon a comparison between the local quality of the contact with various parts of one's own body and the analogous quality of the contact with parts of someone else's body. Assimilation is possible only by means of this twofold exploration. And this is probably one of the processes that enable the blind infant to imitate (to the limited extent that he is able to do so rather tardily). But a blind person *actually touches* the body of others and pays attention to the local quality of the contact, whereas the normal infant does so only rarely. Therefore it is impossible to draw any conclusions from this exposition.

New Aspects of the Problem. Neither of the two hypotheses that we have discussed can give us a satisfactory explanation of imitation. Both are concerned with imaginative creations which, although certainly not inconceivable, are hardly natural, and at any rate are too complicated to be attributed to an infant. Each of the hypotheses is founded on the premise that imitation implies a prior identification with parts of the body, and with positions and movements of both the model and the infant. Is this a valid premise? Isn't it possible that assimilation is the *effect* rather than the *precondition* of initial imitation?

If we give up the idea that the infant, in order to conform to example, must become aware of the similarity between himself and his model, then we can presume that an act may gradually acquire the characteristic features of imitation. Determined at first by an object or an external fact that will impose its form on him, the infant will free himself little by little from the object or fact by yielding, through a series of transferences, to the perception of the model's reaction to this object or fact. We will have to explain how, under special circumstances, this reaction, which at first was merely a signal, becomes inseparable from the model; how awareness of the resemblance can spring from the relationship of contiguity that results from imitation itself.

To justify this hypothesis, we must begin with primary, instinctive reactions, determined by external or internal causes, whose objective similarity in all beings of the same species rests on the uniformity of the inherited systems. We will then describe the associational transferences which beget habits that are subordinate to determinate objects or facts. Last, we will note that perception of the model's act will figure among the causes. The role of such perception, which at first is auxiliary, will increase so greatly that example will become in the end an autonomous principle of activity.

4. THE ORIGINS OF IMITATION

I

General Conformity of Movements and Attitudes. Instincts are characterized by uniformity. Save for a few individual differences, they are also specific. Therefore there will be an objective similarity in the attitudes and acts of individuals, who, independently of one another, behave in identical fashion when subjected to the same causal influences.

This similarity can be observed in *attitudes denoting sensory attention*. Thus, certain objects attract the eye in a way that is almost indistinguishable from the action of a reflex. The direction of one's eyes is drawn to shiny, small objects that appear and move (in the beginning the movements should not be too rapid to be followed by an infant). The same objects attracting the attention of the infant as well as of the adults around him will therefore make the infant's attitude seem to be one of imitation. The direction in which the eyes are focused tallies with the position of the head and body. Any shift of the visual lines from one direction to another is accompanied by a certain deviation of the eyes and head, or even a change in the position of the body. These movements are in no way arbitrary; rather, they are entirely determinate and constant (provided all the movements are free and not restrained by physical or mental exigencies).

The laws that govern these shifts of position and that so exactly regulate the participation of the eyes, head, and body with each successive change are the same for all mankind.

This is also true in regard to the auditory attitude of attention. The head turns; sometimes the entire body turns with it. The infant faces in the direction from which the sound appears to be coming and remains immobilized in this position. Sometimes the head is bent slightly backward, the mouth is open, and the eyes continue to stare in the same direction (L, 3:18).

Other forms of sensitivity — tactile, olfactory, gustatory — likewise have their innate adaptive reactions. In the tactile domain, for example, an innate automatism makes possible the movements that occur when specific organs (hand, finger pads, lips, tongue) are substituted for the gross sensory organs. Accordingly, the observer notes the gesture of touching (L, 2:16), of putting objects in one's mouth (fourth month).

From sensory attitudes we progress toward active behavioral reactions, also innate, as they relate to objects. Examples of such reactions are *locomotion*, with its modal attributes, and *prehension*, with its innumerable derivations that lead to a variety of actions involving objects. I shall not repeat my descriptions of these factors; they were considered earlier when I discussed the theory of instinct.

Spontaneous Progress. Again, it is obvious that the motor suggestions which emanate from objects elicit uniform responses because they address themselves to similarly structured organisms. But I must emphasize the point that the development of these reactions is largely spontaneous. The hesitant, clumsy movements we observed at the start converge toward a definite, standardized model uninfluenced by example.

Hence the difficulty of trying to fix the exact moment when the infant first opposes his thumb. There is no doubt that this positional movement is preformed, but practice is necessary to give it precision. The hand finally discovers the position which, through trial and error, lends efficiency to prehension (L, 2:22). Moreover, progress cannot be made in any other way (L from the end of the first month to the end of the third).

This reasoning can perhaps be applied to more complex cases. I am not at all sure that the progress L made in picking up a pencil (12 months) was due to more accurate observation of the model. With her right hand, well before she was able to do the same thing with the left, she managed to pick up the pencil from the table by holding it between the thumb and the first two fingers. In order to take it with her left hand, she first picked it up with her right hand, then stuck the point of the pencil into the palm of her left hand. Her fingers closed over the pencil (this is the gesture involved in transferring an object from one hand to the other); then she opened the last four fingers, holding the pencil tightly between the inside of her thumb and the edge of her palm. Next, using the tips of her fingers, she grasped the pencil near its point. For several days I watched her as she repeated the maneuver over and over again, about twenty times, acquiring greater speed as she went along. She anticipated each phase of the movement, eliminating unnecessary gestures; finally, without any fumbling and using the appropriate gestures, she managed to pick up the pencil right away. There is not the slightest trace of imitation here; rather, there is the coupling of autonomous progress with the almost unavoidable convergence toward a standard model imposed by the organism.

Let us now investigate another prehensile gesture and the successive stages that lead to its successful execution — taking hold of an object directly and putting it in one's mouth. When the initial gestures are made, the hand, guided by the eyes, is thrust forward but does not reach the object (usually the hand is placed much too low and the movement is not vigorous enough). The hand often remains closed. However, sometimes it is half open (L, 2:3 and 2:5). The back of the hand is upward. The fingers stretch and bend close to the object. Signs of anticipation, which are partly instinctive, will appear more and more regularly, but imitation plays no part. Similarly, when the infant first puts his hand to his mouth, it is usually the back of the hand that first touches his lips. Often the hand goes into the mouth with the object. A little later, he turns his hand the other way before touching his mouth; as a consequence, the fingertips or the objects the infant is holding are the first to come in contact with his lips. A great many examples of this kind of spontaneous development of the instinct can be cited.

The Expression of Emotions. Emotional expression constitutes another category of data whose instinctual origin is beyond question. Let us review a few manifestations of what I might term *primitive mimicry*, which is entirely independent of imitation.

The *smile* in very fleeting form appears quite early; I noticed it on L's second and fifth days of life. The eyes are closed at first, then are opened a little. It is not rare for an infant to smile while sleeping. The corners of the mouth turn up and the eyes narrow. When the smile becomes more pronounced, the mouth opens wide (end of the second month).

The sound of *laughter* at first resembles the crow of a rooster. It is sudden and raucous (L, 1:5; P, end of the second month). At the start of the third month another laugh appears, more like a normal laugh — a series of prolonged outbursts (ha! ha! ha!). Finally, when the infant was eight months old, I noted a giggle. These changes seem to be in no way related to imitation.

Expressions of *astonishment* and *concentration* occur very early. The infant's face takes on a grave look. At times, a vertical line forms on each side of the nose (L, 0:4), at others, the eyebrows are raised (L, 2 months). Sometimes the mouth is opened but often it is closed and the lips are pursed. Immobilized, the infant stares at the object of his attention. Sometimes, too, the mouth closes over the lower lip and the cheeks are a little puffed (P, 4:2).

We can all recognize an expression of *pain* on an infant's face. The forehead is furrowed, the eyes close, the corners of the mouth are turned down, the face reddens, and the mouth opens to form a rectangle. The breath is drawn in and then sharp cries are emitted. By the second month tears make their appearance.

Very early, expressions of *disappointment* or *temper* can be readily distinguished from the other emotions I have just described. When these feelings are expressed, the body is thrust backward, the infant coughs, draws in his breath, and utters a sharp cry, his face red, with white lines close to the nose (P, 3:20). Later, the infant throws the objects he is holding, pounds with his hand, frowns, and stamps his foot (L, 11:11). The intonation of the voice conveys impatience.

Fear is expressed by shuddering, disturbed breathing, opening of the eyes during sleep, fluttering of the eyelids (when the eyes are open), cries, forward thrusts of the arms (L, 0:3).

Desires of every kind are expressed by such things as a characteristic slight coughing (0:10), forward movements of the body, stretching of the limbs (L, 0:9), movements of the tongue (L, 0:16), and secretion of saliva (P, 4 months).

Aversion, on the other hand, is expressed by movements to push the object away (L, 2 months). Gestures signifying rejection take the form of lateral oscillations of the head. They are instinctive in origin (rejection of food or refusal to look at something). Disgust makes the mouth look as if vomiting is about to take place (the lower lip is curled downward).

The arms tremble when certain emotions, such as desire, disappointment, impatience, etc., are keenly felt (L, 22:15).

It is rather difficult at times to form an accurate opinion about certain rather exceptional attitudes that occur late in infancy. However, I am inclined to consider the following gestures to be independent of imitation: L, in a temper, clasps her hands together and then draws them apart violently (23:31). She also hits herself on the head with her hands (L, 11:18) and even pulls her hair. In a burst of a joy, she joins her hands in front of her and rests them on her stomach; her fingers are interlaced, the back of her hand is curved against her arm, etc. I do not believe that she had ever seen anyone make this gesture. It should be remembered that the fact that a gesture occurs late in infancy is not sufficient to allow us to presume that the reaction is not instinctive.

Although the list of examples is not complete, the evidence reviewed here shows that before any imitation exists, before it tends to establish itself spontaneously, there is a uniformity in the behavior of the infant and the adult that is merely a manifestation of the similarity of organs and instincts.

II

Habits and the Role of Experience. It is not part of this task to describe in detail how habits, beginning with these primordial instincts, form and then subordinate the execution of reactions to new perceptions. To give the history of these successive transferences would be an endless task, and I am in a hurry to come to those that interest us particularly.

The principle is always the same. It is always a matter of sensations which, by associating themselves with the acts required by motor sensations, themselves acquire the properties of these motor sensations.

The experience undergone by the infant in his contact with the external world has the effect of subjecting his acts to new perceptions. Reactions increase in variety and become less haphazard. For example, the gesture of picking something up and putting it into one's mouth, at first performed without any discrimination, is gradually limited to *familiar objects* (a spoon, a rattle, a cup, food, etc.) whose special attributes are the determining factor. Reactions to something seen or heard fall into the same category; they occur in response to *familiar* objects that either attract attention or are recognized as a cue of sorts. The entire development of emotional expression is founded on the same principle. Thus the smile, initially a reaction to physical well-being, probably produced by a good digestion or by fondling, will eventually accompany those perceptions that are habitually associated with such states of mind. There is no need to stress these well-known facts. I wish merely to point out that because of the progress occasioned by spontaneous convergence, the infant's behavior comes increasingly to resemble that of the adult.

Training. The child, however, does not grow up exposed to nature alone. From the very first days of life, the influence of the social environment determines in mechanical fashion the forms of the infant's acts and reduces them to a common standard. The infant learns to obey the movement that is conveyed to him. Because such movement is imposed on him initially, he reacts in a passive manner. Soon, however, he begins to participate actively to further the external impetus, and in the end to anticipate it, each phase of the act becoming a cue for the execution of the succeeding one. This learning process takes place at every age level. Its effects are apparent at a very early age, even when the observer makes no effort to elicit them. Later, this educative process guides the child in his acquisition of the power to perform innumerable acts and obviates protracted trial-and-error efforts. It is by means of just such a process that the apprentice, under the guidance of an experienced worker, is initiated into the performance of numerous tasks requiring manual dexterity. Gymnastics and sports also play an important role in the process of learning how to carry out difficult or unusual movements.

It is impossible to state with any degree of accuracy exactly when a child begins to play an active role in the movements involved in dressing and undressing. At first his limbs are lifeless and react only haphazardly; then they passively obey the adult's mechanical urgings. Be that as it may, L reacted perfectly at the age of one and a half. At first she would raise her arms passively when asked to undress. Soon she raised her arms energetically as soon as her dress was touched. She would push her arms into the sleeves immediately upon seeing the opening and her legs would stiffen when her shoes were being put on, etc.

Very early the observer notes the initial movements connected with the holding out of the infant's arms. Upon being seized under the arms, the infant passively moves his arms away from his body. Later, when he realizes that he is about to be picked up, the movement becomes more active.

After the fifth month both children were taught mechanically to play a certain number of little games. First we would guide their hands, then we would associate the movement with a word which became a cue for it. For example, we would say, "good-bye!" (waving our hands); "spank the naughty head!" (hitting our foreheads); "throw a kiss, friend!" (holding out our hands); "happy!" (clapping our hands); "sweetie" (caresses); "naughty!" (touching the palm of one hand with the tip of the index finger of the other hand); "the Spanish dance, the French dance" (we would dance, holding the infant: we raised one arm for the first dance and held the infant's hand for the second); "turn,

turn, little windmill" (turning both hands, one around the other, etc.). All these games were played in succession from the ages of 4:22 to 11:28.

When we held L under her arms, she participated, by leaning to the right and left, in a slow dance whose rhythm she could grasp (6:7).

When she was not yet able to stand alone (6:15), we would hold her hands and help her to stand or sit on command, but she was already contributing a considerable effort of her own. When we held her in our arms, L would hold out an object to someone (9:5). In the same way, she learned to snatch it away as soon as the person was about to take it from her. When she was taking her first steps unaided, she learned, if we held her hands, how to twirl as she danced. At thirteen months she was able to do this unaided. Later, she would ask to be taken on our laps. First we would twirl her around and then seat her on our laps with her feet dangling. When she was one year and eight months, I noticed that as soon as she realized we were going to do this, she would twirl herself and then hold out her arms. This showed that the mechanical training had succeeded before the grown-ups around her realized it.

Interpretation. Mechanical coercion does not operate directly but as a consequence of *suggestion*. Sometimes the infant resists the movement, sometimes he furthers it. But this presupposes at the least that the momentary impetus has been sensed by the infant and that the succeeding phase or tendency of the movement has been anticipated. One has only to try these experiments oneself to realize how difficult it is to keep an arm or a leg completely inert when it is being guided. The indications provided by the tactile and kinesthetic senses are *interpreted* as signs of a tendency. One merely holds oneself in readiness for a quick change of direction if there should be even the slightest resistance on the part of the guide.

But these suggestions will not always be limited to local and instantaneous cues. The infant responds to them with all his instinctual and habitual reactions. To the tug at his hand, the child who can walk (or even if he is as yet unable to do so) will respond not only by an arm movement in the direction indicated but also by leg movements (equilibrium and walking reactions). If I twirl him while holding him by his hands, I suggest the idea of turning, to which he will respond with complicated leg movements. As habit comes to produce more complex coordinated acts, the merest indication will suffice to remind the infant of the entire procedure employed for the execution of a movement. Thus, when P was thirteen months old, he learned to greet people by doffing his cap. The gesture of putting his hand to his head is a familiar one because it is a reminder of earlier acts. Passive movements serve as a brief indication of the timing of a movement and of its connection with other phases of the act. In certain instances, there is occasion for an infant to act on his own, especially if the end to be achieved is suggested to him. The acts I have reviewed here may therefore be regarded as belonging to the category of *self-imitation*, or the process involved in the active search for an interesting effect that has already been experienced.

Research on Subjective Perceptions. In the acts we are about to discuss, suggestion stems from interesting perceptions experienced by the infant rather than from the results of movement. These interesting acts were observed as they were being performed by others, by the infant himself, or through the agency of external objects. A great many factors are involved. Consequently, it is most difficult to give a complete and satisfactory explanation of these acts. Some of them consist of sensory attitudes, locomotion, prehension regulated by an object, or acquired habits employed earlier under similar conditions; others involve the immediate recall of perceptions connected with the objects or the acts themselves. This last factor increasingly exerts its control and, in the course of attempts marked to a greater or lesser degree by haphazard reliance on trial and error, it helps to give the acts their definitive form.

The infant is the object of all kinds of attention. He is dressed and undressed, washed, combed, bathed, and fed. He is also the object of play and fondling. It is quite natural that he should actively attempt to reproduce the characteristic sensations that result from such attention. The following are examples in which this factor plays more or less a part.

P (eight months), placing his index finger on his lips, tried to reproduce the effect we obtained when we interrupted a continuous sound he was emitting. We did this by waving our hands rapidly in front of his mouth. The localization of this gesture was determined by tactile sensation.

He learned to blow through his nose. We would hold a handkerchief to his nose and say, "Blow your nose." Thereupon he himself put the handkerchief to his face (tactile as well as visual sensations). The same tactile sensations intervened in the act of pinching his own nose or ear after we had done so; or in learning to comb and brush his hair (11:13). He tried to put on his socks and shoes. He placed the shoe near the tip of his foot or alongside it and pulled the sock up on his leg (1 year and 2 days; visual and tactile sensations). He could, upon request, point to his big tooth; that is, he would place his hand on the part of his mouth we had just touched.

I would balance him on my knee or on my outstretched leg, saying, "Trot, gallop!" He would stand up and reproduce the same movement by bending his knees, then standing up again. I call the reader's attention to the fact that all the infant's movements differed from one another, with the exception of the act of balancing vertically the upper part of his body. The interesting sensations were reproduced by the infant's own efforts (14 months).

Having seen us do it, P tried to remove his socks by pulling them from his toes. He could locate the place to pull but was not yet able to imitate the movement. He managed to put a thimble on his finger. He tried to cut his nails after watching me do so. The visual and tactile localization of the hand serving as the *object* in relation to the scissors was fairly accurate; but the localization of the scissors in relation to the hand serving as the *agent* was not (14:22).

The following are analogous examples observed in our second child: L (9:5) learned to use her small hairbrush. She also learned to put on her bonnet (9:15); guided by tactile sensations, she would place it against her temple but not on her head. When she was a year old, she was able to put it on her head properly. She washed her forehead with a washcloth changing hands for each side of the head (her own idiosyncrasy, 10:15). She could put bath powder on her chest and lower abdomen with a powder puff (11:20), blow her nose, and wipe the corners of her mouth (12:24), etc.

Research on Objective Results. Objects as well as their displacement figure in the preceding examples. In the following ones, they occupy a major place, and it is obvious that they are connected with the general prehensile reaction. Thus, when P (3:33 [*sic*] 3:30) and L (4:8), put their hands on the piano keys after watching me play, they were actually attempting to seize these mobile, shiny, sonorous objects. The same kind of movement was involved when P tried to catch the ball I threw to him (9:28); or when he took a pencil I had given him and banged it on the sheet of paper (9:21). Far more than the gesture of the hand, the movement of the object drew his attention. We often see a young child fling himself on a marble, a ball, or a mechanical toy and seize it. He does not play with it and soon lets it fall, completely indifferent. Later, the object itself will interest him. The transformations and displacements of an object, or the relations of several objects to one another, attract the child's attention far more than any human action that intervenes as a causative agent. According to a general law, the real target is the *result* rather than the means by which an act is carried out. The means are discovered through trial and error — in other words, by a determinism that results from habits established earlier.

Thus, having watched me write, P (9:21) picks up the pencil

(at first with his whole hand) and bangs it on the paper. Then, when he accidentally grasps it near the point, he manages to turn the pencil around. This does not appear to be an imitation of the relation of the hand to the pencil but rather an attempt to copy the relation of the point to the paper. Later on he no longer bangs the pencil. Instead, he uses it to make broad strokes on the paper. He is trying to reproduce the result, the lines, the effect of the pencil on the paper rather than the movement or the position of the hand. By this time, to be sure, hands — not only his own but also the hands of others — have become familiar *objects* to the infant. It is altogether possible that he is trying to imitate attitudes and movements, guided by the visible similarity of appearance and form. Although I do not categorically exclude this hypothesis, I am inclined to think that the sight of a pencil moving across a piece of paper and leaving marks on it directly evokes a prehensile tendency and an inclination to achieve this effect on the object. A rolling ball causes the infant to hold out his hand, whereas a dog will attempt to trap the object with its teeth and a cat with its claws. Instinct dictates the gesture; habits acquired by trial and error account for its continuation; and its final form is determined by the influence of the *objective result* suggested as a model, with the latter gradually giving the gesture the requisite form to attain the result.

In the following acts, which I will cite without comment, the objects and their relationships are of prime importance. P (10:13) tries to knit. He holds the needle in one hand and passes it to his other hand under the wool thread (relation of needle to thread). Later (11:18), he tries to wind the thread around the needle. Other activities include washing clothes in a tub (11:25); using a piece of bread to soak up the gravy on his plate; striking a match against the matchbox and taking it to the gas heater (12:3); stirring the fire with an iron poker (12:13); sweeping, dusting, drying the dishes; taking paper from a wastepaper basket and tossing it in the fire (12:18); putting a key in a lock (12:23); attempting (unsuccessfully) to button his shoes with a button hook (15:7); trying to kill a fly with a folded newspaper (17 months); ironing an article of clothing (18:15); putting wood in the fireplace (13:13); eating soup with a spoon (14:2); putting a candle in the candle holder, all the while correcting his mistakes by inserting one piece at a time (14:20); taking money from a purse and handing it to someone (15 months); drawing lines on the ground with a stone; putting the ball in the hole of a cup-and-ball game (using a movement that is of course very different from that of the model) (14:7); putting a needle into a narrow tube (11:23), etc.

In other instances, the aim is not to place two objects together; rather, modification of the object by the movement is the result the infant seeks to reproduce. Examples of this include leafing through a book (12:13); opening a drawer or a door already half open, shelling a pea (13 months); opening and closing the lid of a box (13:9); opening an umbrella by pushing out the ribs (notice how the means employed by the infant differ from those used by the model; this proves that the infant's attention is focused mainly on the result. (Employing habitual and *general* means, the infant makes no effort to imitate the special means of the model, which he does not grasp.) Sometimes the interesting result is an auditory perception: shaking a toy bell to hear the sound (8 months); turning a little musical windmill (failure at 11:20, success at 11:25).

Similarly, my records show our second child seizing a pencil with her whole hand and banging on paper with the point, or drawing lines (L, 9:25). She often holds the pencil horizontally in her clenched hand as she moves it over the paper. She tries to place the pencil closer to the paper instead of turning her wrist or changing the position of the pencil in her hand. She presses her hand as hard as she can on the table, but this of course produces no result whatsoever (an absurd personal mannerism).

She attempts (unsuccessfully) to light the electric lamps (10:15); rolls a ball (10:15); uses a hairbrush; throws an object into the air (11:10); rubs a match on a matchbox (11:12); dips a pencil in the inkwell (after having seen someone dip a pen in it); dips a rag in a pail of water and washes the floor (11:12); plays with marbles or with a ball (12 months); washes clothes by rubbing one part against the other (12:24); twirls a pencil between her fingers (she cannot continue the movement by changing the position of her fingers; she has observed only the movement of twirling the pencil, not the way the fingers change position — 13 months).

III

Subordination to Example: Sensory Attitudes. These last-mentioned acts tally with a certain definition of imitation. The imitation does not comprise *all the movements* involved but rather the *effects* of the act. These obvious elements are the only ones common to both the model and the copy. Therefore, in the example offered, they retain the significance they had in the infant's spontaneous games.

Thus, as the infant's motor experience grows and becomes more and more diversified, he sees in the acts suggested by others an increasing number of effects produced by his own activity. This recognition results from the fact that the range of his own activities has been enriched by new acquisitions.

At the same time, the infant will better observe the *model's movements*, and these, which are devoid of motor properties, derive significance from the efficient elements with which they are associated. And here we come to true imitation. Instinctive reactions and habits acquired by some sort of process are already, as we have seen, definite in form. If there is to be true imitation, there has to be a transition from their subordination to the object (or to the special cue that determines them) to subordination to the *example* offered by the model.

In a first group of data, *an auxiliary object* regulates both the attitude of the model and that of the infant. Then, since perception of the movements of the model has, through association, acquired motor properties, it retains them, even in the absence of the object, whose educative role is terminated.

Remarkable examples of this are the sensory responses, above all the movement of the eyes. As we have seen, the same objects attract the eyes of the infant and those of the people around him. This uniformity in the movement of the eyes toward interesting objects is something that occurs at every moment. Therefore, it ultimately lends to the movements of the head and eyes of others the significance of a cue indicating the presence of an object in a given direction. In fact, all children more or less acquire the habit of looking wherever they see other people look.

Often one either walks toward the object perceived or reaches out a hand toward it. These movements help to direct the infant's eyes toward the object. As a consequence of the law of anticipation, the infant learns to obey the indications of other people's eyes without waiting for further confirmation.

But, generally speaking, a special learning process, altogether spontaneous, also furthers this transference. We teach the infant to look in the direction in which we point a finger or move a hand. The hand, especially if it is not entirely immobile, is one of the particular objects that quite naturally attract the infant's attention. Once he looks, he eventually notices the object to which the hand is pointing. At first one has to stand quite close to the infant. Later, instead of guiding him by the hand alone, we accustom him to seeking the object indicated by an outstretched arm. In all these movements the individual indicating the location of the object is also looking in the direction he designates. This additional cue is also helpful to the infant, who has already learned to interpret hand gestures.

The entire learning process is rather complex. The model indicates only one direction in which the object should be sought, at an indeterminate distance from the infant. Unfortunately, not until quite late in the infant's development did it occur to me to make these habits the subject of precise experimentation. By the beginning of the twenty-second month, I found that such habits had already been perfected. Watching me, the child looked in the same direction: up, down, to the right, to the left, with or without movements of the head or hand. Probably he had learned to do so a good deal earlier. According to the findings of another study, an infant at seven months was able to find someone rather far away by following the direction of a pointed finger. B. Perez even cites a three-month-old girl (?) who looked in the same direction as the grown-ups around her. Such examples of imitation are particularly instructive. Can they be explained differently? The infant, because he is able to see, knows nothing about his eyes or their movements. How can he imitate the eye movements of other people?

Since he lacks knowledge of vision, are we to assume tactile or kinesthetic knowledge? Awareness of such movements occurs only when the eyes move in a certain way. This kind of general perception of and by itself will not impinge upon an infant's attention. It seems to play no part in determining the direction of his gaze, which, on the contrary, is governed by remarkable visual, auditory, or tactile sensations. We have just seen how certain visible objects — the eyes or the hands of others — acquire in this instance a regulatory power because of the habitual specialization of a general reaction, which is due to multiple transferences. The attitude of the instructor determines that of the infant, but not because of the resemblance of the two. The infant is as yet unaware of this similarity because one of the factors required for making a comparison is lacking in his consciousness. Moreover, the infant's attitude becomes efficient only when it replaces the action of the object. It is merely a cue of sorts.

Can it be that the sight of the model acquires motor properties because of an accidental contiguity? Actually, one cannot term accidental the fact that the same objects attract the attention of both the infant and the adult. Nor is it accidental that the adult is the most important object to attract the infant's attention. (The "accident" is so inevitable that even domesticated animals — dogs, for example — are able to obey indications of this kind.) For the infant, the adult becomes "the measure of all things," a special object whose gestures have a particular significance. The adult is the universal intermediary between the infant and the world. Imitation of the direction in which other people look represents one aspect of the infant's dependence on the adult and, in general, on the interdependence that binds all members of society.

This comment will permit us to survey quickly the other sensory attitudes which lend themselves to the same kind of analysis. The infant is as unaware of the attitude of auditory attention, at least in its visible aspects, as he is of the attitude of visual attention; but in reacting to sound, he also observes the mimicry of other people, which becomes a cue for the act of listening. The same is true of all his other attitudes. The role of the object becomes obscured by that of example. Sensory attitudes, as the reader will recall, entail certain general attitudes that are interdependent. The consequence of this is that behavior in relation to objects will be regulated by the attitude of others and will thus become *independent of a real, actually given object.*

General Bodily Displacements. It has already been pointed out that general movements of the body (locomotion, orientation) are regulated by interesting objects and only secondarily by the attitude of other people toward them. But more direct forms of relationship exist between the imitator and the model. From the start, the adult is the most important object for the infant (for example, his mother or nurse). The result is that movements are oriented, as soon as they become possible, in such a way as to appear to be a kind of imitation (following or looking for someone). This orientation becomes in turn a precondition of more definite imitations (regulating one's step to that of the person one is following; assuming the same position as the adult in relation to objects — all of which serve to regulate subsequent acts). Not only does the act of following appear in its utilitarian aspect; it can also assume the instinctive form of play. This brings it even closer to true imitation because it is now merely a matter of pretending, and the parallelism of movements which was heretofore only a means can now become an end. Inversely, to turn around and flee from someone who is pursuing is also a primordial instinctive reaction which likewise can become the principle of a game. When children begin to run, their great pleasure is to chase others and to be chased themselves, with each movement of the partner determining that of the child.

This is nothing more than the acting out of elementary instincts. Animals play together in this way; some, such as dogs and monkeys, also play with people.

Seen differently, an adult's movement likewise lends itself to direct imitation because of its rhythmic quality. We assume, of course, that such movement becomes localized and also definite in form. We have already noted that L (6:7) actively identified herself with the rhythm of swaying which we had imprinted. At 10:13 she imitated spontaneously the swaying movement of nursing mothers as they rock their babies, balancing herself first on one foot and then on the other. Unable as yet to walk, she merely retained the notion of a rhythmic movement. Sitting on a chair, she swayed to and fro. P (16:22) would fall into step with other children, each holding on to the one in front of him. He moved as they did, emphasizing the stamp of the feet. This act combines following with the adoption of a motor rhythm.

Thus, in all these examples, we observe a uniformity of attitudes and movements, because here man (who is, on occasion, an animal) is himself the object that is prey to the urgings of rather general instinctive tendencies. In this way he comes to form habits that in their particulars perfect the notion of integrating movements.

Movements of the Mouth. Speech, as noted above, is a kind of intermediary object that lends itself to direct imitation, whereas the movements of the mouth do not. Vocal imitation prepares

the way for the imitation of movements, whose visual perception in the end becomes motor, independently of sound. In
fact, imitation of facial expressions comes later, long after
imitation of sound, with which it seems to be connected. The
first example of facial imitation noted in L (14:15) is an imitation of the following grimace which she has seen her brother
make: the mouth is opened wide, the cheeks are sucked in, the
lips rounded as if to say "oh." She actually began by saying "oh."
(This is the game of imitating an idiot or a devil.) Later (16
months), the grimace becomes a silent one. Perhaps sound plays
a similar role in the imitation of movements of the tongue (as
if to say *âââ* or *l ll*), or in the act of pouting (*m m m* . . .), etc.
Actually, when we wish to designate a lip or tongue movement,
we characterize it by sounds that tally with the pronunciation
that should be given to it. Again, when we blow a whistle or
a horn, it is probably the auxiliary role of sound that we are
seeking. The infant puts the instrument in his mouth and at
first imitates the sound with his voice instead of blowing. The
noise doubtless facilitates the localization of the gesture; later,
this becomes unnecessary. Similarly, L (7:19) puts some flowers
in her mouth, imitating with her mouth, in deliberately exaggerated manner, the sound people make when they sniff flowers.
I have noted that a child, when about to blow his nose, will
hesitate, not knowing whether to use his mouth or nose. Once
the act is correctly performed, it is the visible shape of the nose
in the model that takes precedence over sound and becomes
independent of its influence.

The act of putting something in one's mouth is connected,
on the other hand, with the sensory and alimentary function.
The infant sees those around him put familiar objects in their
mouths (bread, cake, candy, or cups, glasses, and spoons); this
stimulates the same habit in him. Here again, sooner or later,
the association is inevitable. It is understandable that playing
with an infant or taking care of him should further his performance of the act. The mother or nurse tastes every spoonful
of soup she gives an infant to make sure it is not too hot. The

infant watches this merry-go-round impatiently. The spoon goes from the lips of the adult to his own, or else the adult pretends to feed the soup to some imaginary infant, etc. The result is that the visible shape of the mouth acquires the power to direct the gesture of the hand. L (7:10) begins to put the spoon in her mouth; at 9:10 she *imitates* the gesture of putting her index finger in her mouth; at 9:25 she offers to put in other people's mouths the candy she has put in her own. The infant Scupin (61) observed would not remain quiet when he saw someone put a glass to his lips until he too was given a cup (5:26). He opened his mouth when he saw someone drinking (6:15). The effect of the drinking glass is probably more important than the act of drinking itself, but drinking will in turn become significant.

Gestures of the Hand. Gestures indicating direction are derived from prehension. The infant holds his hand out toward an object, even one that is placed too far from him. An adult intervenes and hands it to him. The gesture of taking hold of something therefore becomes transformed into a gesture that demands something. This is followed by a gesture to designate the object requested or by one to designate the object the infant has in mind but is not requesting — in other words, a gesture to attract the attention of others. We too make this same gesture when we wish to draw the infant's attention to the object. He seeks it in the direction indicated by us and then he in turn points to it. L (22 months) holds her hand in the direction I have designated and asks: "There?" Thus, the mere sight of a gesture indicating a direction produces and directs the infant's similar gesture toward a real or imaginary object.

We may generalize here about this concept. The infant learns to exert his influence on objects *whenever* our own activity produces interesting changes in them. But the perception of this activity will soon become the cue for reactions relating to the object. If the infant's way of holding a pencil is not really acquired by imitation, as we have shown, but rather perfected through trial and error and therefore associated first of all with the sight of the pencil, then it follows that this manner of holding the pencil, which the child has mastered, cannot in turn become subordinate to the sight of the position of the model's hand. The time therefore comes when the position of the model's hand can be *copied* without any assistance from the object.

Just as the act is freed from the influence of the *object*, so it becomes independent of the *cue* upon which it initially depended. This is true of all acts that are learned mechanically. When, for example, the infant learns to wave his hand to say good-bye, the cues are at first the kinesthetic or tactile indications of the movement, then the word, good-bye, and finally the circumstances usually associated with the gesture (leaving a room). But everybody responds to the infant's gesture; we all invite it by waving good-bye in a similar fashion. It is the sight of this gesture that in turn becomes the stimulus.

I would like to stress one example that will serve to clarify this point. The infant learns to shake hands. At first, you take his hand and shake it, saying, "Friend!" Later, the infant holds out his hand when someone wants to shake hands with him; at the same time he says, "Friend." Finally, the gesture alone suffices. In the same way we teach a dog to give us his paw and he learns this easily. Can one maintain that the dog is imitating with his paw the gesture of the outstretched hand? In the infant the symmetry is far more perfect; yet this is only accidental. The outstretched hand constitutes some sort of cue; in the beginning, the psychological mechanism is not very different in an infant and in an animal. Thereafter, however, the act becomes subordinate to the sight of a similar act performed by others.

The illustration cited above can be stated in general terms. Long before example begins to serve as the initiator of new acts, we "show" the infant the act we are asking him to perform. But we teach it to him by more efficient means (objective effects obtained through trial and error; action directed passively). In thereby associating efficient means with demonstration by example, we confer a motor significance upon the example.

Training through Selection. A most curious form of this kind of social conditioning of an infant's acts is what we might term the *selection* of the spontaneous movements by those living with the infant. In the beginning we encourage the infant to act by using means that are entirely inappropriate for helping him to perfect the act we are encouraging him to execute. We speak to him in a language that he cannot understand. Only our intonation or the gestures that accompany what we say can have a generally stimulating effect on him. We touch the area involved or passively produce a movement. When, in the course of these maneuvers, during which a mother must exercise a good deal of patience, a result is accidentally obtained, we reward the infant with sweets, caresses, laughter, or signs of approval and admiration. If one particular example is present among all the stimuli, we do not at first realize that it is more efficient than any of the others. But once the result has been obtained, it tends to be closely associated with the example, which then becomes the cue.

This, I believe, is how many precocious "imitations" should be interpreted. For example, in Scupin's notes (61) we read that around the eleventh week the infant acquires the habit of putting his tongue between his lips. One day, the mother herself imitates the infant, who has just done this. Several times she urges the infant: "Stick your little tongue out too!" If one repeats this over and over again, in the end one obtains the desired result among other grimaces and mischievous looks. Completely amazed, the mother naturally repeats the experiment until she is satiated. After a few hours of sleep the infant wakes up and immediately sticks out his tongue when asked to do so. He does it again when the mother combines her request with the act of sticking out her own tongue. It should be noted that the infant has already acquired the habit of making this facial gesture. The mother takes advantage of the moment when the infant first does it and seems inclined to repeat it. In the course of the mental excitation created by this scene, speech and example quickly acquire a character in which example plays a part no more important than that of speech. There is nothing here, therefore, that leads one to think that the infant assimilates the model with the imitation. Rather, the phenomenon involved is one of selection. Animal trainers very frequently make use of it.

It is plain, however, that this type of learning, like all processes that depend on a movement guided by the teacher, has something contingent and artificial about it. In the history of imitation, such phenomena play only a *secondary* role. Although they do accelerate the process involved in learning how to execute movements, they are not essential to the process itself. In this instance, social pressure produces precocious manifestations which, although not always continuous, will inevitably appear someday in one way or another. We have seen that in a situation of constraint, or in one involving some kind of mechanical training, such manifestations merely indicate the path the infant will later follow as a consequence of self-imitation.

IV

Symbolic Imitation. The infant's acts, at first subordinate to the object or to the situation to which they respond, gradually free themselves from this dependence and instead become increasingly subordinate to acts performed by the model in relation to this object or situation. One special form of imitation throws some light on this transformation and denotes a certain stage of development. This is what we might term *symbolic* imitation. It is a sketch, a pretense, an evocative gesture, a feint rather than a copy. It is addressed to an imaginary object, or if the object is actually present, the act is merely suggested. This proves that a gesture is not merely an instinctive or habitual response. The idea of the act is now present, and it possesses a certain autonomy. This characteristic is to be found not only in acts suggested by the example of others or by speech but also in those that result from self-imitation.

Symbolic imitation develops primarily in the course of the second or third year. The following are a few illustrative examples: When L (11:10) calls the red point of my elbow a nipple, I tell her she can suck it. Thereupon she imitates the act of sucking; she begins to laugh, however, and does not actually put her lips to my elbow. At the same age she pretends to put a marble in her mouth immediately after she has been forbidden to do so. She smacks her lips defiantly. As a game to frighten us (12:8), she imitates the way a dog walks and barks, probably because she has seen her brother doing it. At 15:14 she pretends to be ill and lies down on her bed, moaning. At twenty-one months, at my request she imitates a train, an automobile, a boat; she thrusts herself forward, her eyes wide open and staring, and says "Hou!" At twenty-two months she shows her mother a square of paper and tells her it is a little wagon, inviting her to climb up on it. When her mother consents, she becomes silent and then disappears in order to avoid carrying out an unrealizable suggestion, which is merely a form of pretending.

This kind of symbolic activity is also evident in the first drawings, which date from the same period (22 months). As yet L is capable of drawing only shapeless lines. But with a stroke of the pencil on an incomplete sketch, she indicates the place where the details that are lacking belong (parts of the human face). At this time, she also begins to tell little stories that are very brief imitations of tales her brother or mother has told her.

The following are some other examples of P's activities. At 12:13 he imitates an act to describe what he is alluding to. To ask someone to give him his horn, which is in the next room, he puts his hand to his mouth and imitates the sound. At 15:18, when we ask him to throw a stone, he makes the gesture of throwing, even though he does not have a stone in his hand. Upon seeing a baby cry, he imitates the gesture of giving it the breast (16:22). He pretends he is a beggar; bent over on a cane, he asks for a penny (15:8); or he imitates a car by pulling his shoes along the floor by their laces. He pretends to remove a flea from an infant's head, then throws it away or crushes it with his nails (we were in Algeria at the time — 16:22). He pretends to be ill or imitates the mailman, the laundress, the butcher. All this play consists of imaginary elements or of real objects to which a symbolic and conventional significance is given (18:10). Holding a long stick, he pretends to knock down lemons from an imaginary tree. He offers us "pretend" cakes or candy. He pretends to wash clothes, using a book for a washboard (21 months). Each day the games he plays increase in complexity and imitative skill. For example, at twenty-three months he pretends he is a butcher. A whole series of imaginary activities ensue. These include blowing his horn; turning a part on his car that is supposed to be the brake; getting out to open up the trunk and take out the meat; sharpening his knife; cutting off a piece of meat and removing the bone, holding his knife in the center and using the point; handing over the meat and collecting payment for it.

These examples will suffice as illustrations. During the third year the games become increasingly varied and frequent. This marks the start of the most attractive stage in a child's development. In books dealing with children, almost all the descriptions of play refer largely to this period. What interests me particularly at this point is *the emancipation of the act from the object*. Such liberation initially determines to a considerable extent the characteristics of the imitated gesture, its autonomy, and the growing role played by detailed observation of the model's movements.

Pure Imitation. As a result of this educative process the child learns to imitate a *movement* or an *attitude*, even a meaningless gesture. He begins by imitating a *significant act*, which is characterized by the performance of a function whose objective elements play an essential role — one that enables the subject to compare his perception of his own acts with those of the model. At this stage, objects are relegated to a secondary role. The place they formerly held is taken by *pure* imitation, which may be described as a kind of *residuum* of the act's function. Thus, this pure imitation occurs rather late in the child's development.

It would be meaningless, of course, to attempt to establish too rigorous a chronology for this phenomenon or to try to distinguish fixed periods. Certain movements have become easy to imitate by detaching themselves from acts that relate to objects; other movements, which have already reached this stage, become part of the ensemble of complex, significant acts the child imitates by combining each of them with its simple elements. What we have here is a simultaneous, twofold activity consisting of analysis and synthesis; but analysis occurs first.

We can, to be sure, adduce examples of pure imitation that occur early: L imitating the dance of the puppets (6:27), opening and closing her hand, or waving it to say good-bye; P (8 months) hitting himself on the head or shaking his finger in warning; L (8 months) raising her arm; L sticking out her tongue (7:22) or closing her eyes (12 months), etc. But these are games taught the infant in a variety of ways (passive movements, selection, etc.); the imitations are not spontaneous, or else they are visible acts that can be directly compared to those of the model.

Some experiments — this is scarcely surprising — are doomed to failure. For example, at nine months L is already able to imitate the gesture of brushing her hair. She brushes her own and ours, moving with ease from one gesture to another. Yet twenty days later she cannot imitate the gesture of placing her hand on top of her head. The localization of the last part of this movement is not yet entirely independent of the object (the hairbrush). The process of abstraction, so far as the gesture is concerned, has not been completed. At 9:25 L is unable to imitate the movement of putting her hand to her ear. At the start of her thirteenth month I tested her a few times on imitating a few easy acts, which she managed to perform right away —

raising the arm vertically, for instance. Once she was able to understand what I expected of her, I suggested entirely new gestures. For example: thumbing one's nose, or crossing one's arms on one's chest. She was quite disconcerted. By the beginning of the third year, in spite of repeated testing, she did not even attempt to thumb her nose; a little later she succeeded in crossing her arms. However, although L was willing and concentrated all her attention on what she was doing, her analysis of the position of the hands remained altogether inadequate.

The following are examples of pure imitation that occurred in the course of the second year. P (16:22) imitated his friends' special way of walking, exaggerating their mannerisms as he did so. L (22 months) successfully performed the following experiments the very first time or after some slight hesitation: raised her arms to shoulder level without bending them, sideways or straight ahead of her; from this position, she brought her forearms to a vertical position, or put her hands on her shoulders. She raised her leg, either keeping it stiff or bending the knee. She leaned forward, backward, or to the side. She bent her knees and put her hands on her hips. She bent her head forward and backward, and turned it to the right and to the left. At 22:23 she tried to imitate the way her brother jumped, flexing her legs but getting only as far as the first position. She managed to imitate fairly well walking on all fours (the foot and the opposite arm were raised at the same time). She also imitated the deliberately comic way her brother walked (23:12), bending over backward as far as possible, her stomach stuck out; or the position of a seated person who crosses his legs; or finally, an infant who puts a thumb in his mouth and the other hand to his ear.

Imitative mimicry develops in the same way. Actually, during the period to which we have limited our observations, this played only a secondary role. The infant reacts to his own emotions by means of a spontaneous mimicry that owes nothing to imitation but which can, as we have seen, be subordinate to certain facial expressions of others. However, the infant is scarcely independent of the affective state itself. This kind of spontaneous mimicry can be gradually influenced by a grimace that stems from other motor functions and constitutes a voluntary and modifiable element of such functions. I never noticed anything of this kind in our older child during the first twenty-five months. But I did observe in the younger, after the fifteenth month, several examples of spontaneous mimicry which were obviously the result of her older brother's example. For instance, at 14:15, she imitated a facial expression (rounded mouth with cheeks either puffed out or drawn in). At twenty-two and a half months, I noticed a series of poses and grimaces, likewise due to her brother's example, that had to do with playing with puppets: turning the head quickly to the left and the right with a mechanical stiffness; standing suddenly stock still, eyes staring, face turned upward, chin thrust forward, and the head turned to one side; or a very affected expression of pleasure or desire (for example, when something good to eat is brought in): the head right, the neck swollen, eyes open wide, hands in front, open, trembling with excitement. This is a mixture of imitative and spontaneous elements that are also to be found in the affected, exaggerated expressions which are naturally furthered by the environment. At twenty-six months she knew how to "make big eyes." The voice and its intonations are the essential factors in these imitations, because they are, par excellence, the most imitable.

Whereas in the young child "pretend" pure imitation of affective attitudes does not attain its finished form, the development of sensory attitudes is more complete. When L was thirty-two months old, I suggested that she imitate the following movements (by telling her, "Do as I do"): "Turn your eyes to the right, to the left, up, down, and keep your head still." She did this rather quickly. We must note, however, that in her first attempts she turned both *her eyes and her head*; then she corrected herself. What better proof do we need that pure imitation comes after imitation of similar significant acts?

Let us return to the examples cited above. First there was

regulation of the *gaze* by the interesting object; then, by the gesture that designated it; next, by the gaze of others, which constitutes a new cue, so that all the visual attention of others becomes the cue for an indeterminate object to be looked for in a certain direction. Finally, the child no longer expects to see anything. He no longer asks, "There?" as he did during the test made at twenty-two months. It is only now that the movement is finally copied as a movement. This is the final stage of an entire evolution and can only be understood as such. Naturally, even after the child reaches a higher level, the beginning and intermediate stages remain. All these movements correspond to different situations. In cases of pure imitation, the infant's state of mind is not the same as it is for an interested pseudoimitative reaction; but the one has become possible only because of the other.

If we were to follow this evolution to the end of the second year or above all to the third year, we would come to gestures that *describe* the shape, size, movements, and changes of an object. It was not until L was thirty-six and a half months old that, in speaking of a large orange, she puffed up her cheeks to give us an idea of its size. At the same age, she noticed a sudden flickering in the intensity of light shed by an electric lamp, caused by a faulty connection. She imitated this by blinking her eyes several times. During the first months of the third year, gestures appeared that indicated measurement of dimensions. "As big as that," she would say, raising her hand to a certain height from the floor; or, "as fat as this," and she would hold her hands a certain distance apart. At thirty-eight months she used her hand to imitate a *vertical* movement made by the wooden horses on a merry-go-round. A little later she used a similar movement to describe the way the merry-go-round *turned*. She portrayed, by a trembling of her hands, the movement of waves produced by the propeller of a tugboat.

Symbolic imitation and the imitation of meaningless gestures or of an object develop late and therefore represent the most evolved forms of imitation. They seem to be entirely *human* and take us far from the realm of instinctive reactions.

Conclusion. Let us attempt to draw a general conclusion from this lengthy review of the data, which may have seemed tedious.

In rejecting the lazy hypothesis of a special instinct to explain imitation, we must connect imitation with primordial forms of activity. The perception of example is efficient only because, according to the principle laid down by Delacroix, "Visual perception . . . affects and releases a function or a group of functions" (20). Constituted functions (prehension, locomotion, sensory adaptations, etc.) rather than elementary movements are stimulated by perception. Imitation culminates solely in a transference that occurs at times directly, at other times by means of a training of sorts, to which the structure of instincts and of society gives a general direction that is in no way accidental. Imitation is not determined by the object but rather by the act of a human model; and finally, by the very movements that constitute the act.

Imitation is not a universal form of infantile activity. Although powerful factors operate to subordinate the infant's conduct to that of his fellow beings rather than to the direct influences of the physical environment, such influences do not always tend to produce a conformity in behavior. It is therefore necessary for us at this point to investigate how limited is the group of imitations created by general reactions, and how they are defined. In other words, we must describe the infant's state of mind when he imitates, and the consciousness of imitation which he acquires.

AWARENESS
OF
IMITATION

I

Objective Knowledge about the Human Form. Imitation is not complete until it is accompanied by the awareness that one is imitating, by the notion of one's own resemblance to other beings, and by the knowledge that one's acts are equivalent to those of others. In examining this subject, we will begin by demonstrating what it means to an infant to know other people.

The first indications of an infant's awareness of other human beings are almost impossible to detect because they occur so early. When an infant is no more than three days old, his manifestations of surprise and attention seem to be more pronounced in the presence of people than in the presence of mere objects. From the ninth to the eleventh day, as illustrated in the case of L, this becomes indisputable. An infant's observable reactions include serious attention, a fleeting smile, and movements in the direction of the nearby person accompanied by a general state of agitation. There is no need to emphasize the associations that lend interest to this perception; the perception of familiar individuals quickly becomes the center of the infant's affective life.

When is an infant able to differentiate *visually* among the people familiar to him? (This question has already been discussed in connection with hearing.) The difficulty here is one of isolating the perceptions of the various sensory organs.

When L was sixteen days old she behaved quite differently when her mother (who breast-fed her) held her than she did when I or her nurse did. She was much more agitated in her mother's arms; she coughed (desire to suck), fell asleep less readily, etc. Although in this instance the role of vision was not clear, the same was not true of P (2:22). He plainly differentiated between the people he knew and strangers; the latter he rejected by crying whereas he held out his arms to his mother, the nurse, or myself (the same was true of L at 2:5). By the following month the circle of familiar faces had grown larger. The infant's attitude toward strangers was quite different from his attitude toward neighbors or friends (P, 3:9; L, 3:28). Nor should one neglect the role of a combination of factors — time, place, etc. L, who recognized me easily when I was in my usual place, about two meters away from her, did not recognize me when I went to the park to see her (2:5). Around the fourth month, the children expressed either desire or reluctance to be taken into one person's arms when held by another (L, 3:28; P, 3:22 and 3:29).

In any case, at that stage in the children's development, the general appearance of the human form was something altogether familiar to them. From a distance of approximately sixteen meters, P recognized people on a balcony even though they were surrounded by many objects. He smiled at these people and held out his arms.

In the human form, the infant's attention is attracted by the face, and above all by the eyes and mouth. Later we will cite indirect evidence of this. The location of the breast is recognized at an early age, and this is connected with visual clues. Both L (2:6) and P (2:9), lying on their mother's lap, turned their heads toward the breast (which was concealed) and tried to raise themselves up in order to reach it. When L (2:6) was being held in her mother's arms, she leaned over to reach her mother's breast. P (2:17) demonstrated the role played by vision. Placed in the nursing position, he began to make sucking movements but did not try to take the breast until he saw it. L (3:28) tried to thrust her head into the opening of her mother's dress. When both children were approximately the same age, I noticed the impression made upon them by the sight of a stranger nursing her baby (L, 4:8; P, 3:24). P immediately wanted his mother, and L asked to be carried over to the nursing mother, whereupon she seized the woman's breast with both her hands.

In the first games infants play with others, their attention may be especially attracted to other kinds of details. L (3:28), who was beginning to seize objects she saw, was particularly prone to grab people's hair, their beards (4:8), their fingers (4:19), and their clothing (4:21). When I imitated the movement of puppets, etc., she watched my hands very closely. An enumeration of the data on developments that occur prior to the fifth month would make tedious reading. In demonstrating the way visual perception becomes the regulator of certain acts, we have shown indirectly how an infant's attention is drawn to the various parts of the human body.

The Scope of Objective Imitation. On the other hand, it is interesting to note that very early in an infant's development this objective knowledge of the human body can be characterized by the way it lends itself to abstract thought. Many animals react when they see themselves in a mirror. None however, react to their likeness in a drawing, in a piece of sculpture, or in a photograph.[1] In the fifth month P (4 months and 4:5) seemed to be interested in a photographic reproduction of Franz Hals's *Head of a Child* (the head is life-size and very expressive). He smiled and waved his arms, but his reaction was somewhat indecisive. Two weeks later he was apparently quite indifferent to the picture. His sister was to behave in the same way at the same age (4:11). But in her sixth [*sic*] month (6:12) she not only showed an interest in the painting but also in a terra cotta bust (the life-size head of a woman). Her brother (6:15) laughed when he saw pictures of people: he seized them and kissed them (life-size or smaller), especially a small colored religious picture, two large figures of women painted on a calendar, and a full-length portrait of several children. From 7:15 to eight months, P definitely reacted to snapshots. To make sure of this,

1. Köhler's experiments do, however, prove that the *chimpanzee* recognizes objects in a photograph.

I played a game with him to which he was accustomed (making the sound *brr* by rubbing his finger against his lips, causing them to vibrate; stroking my cheeks when I said, "Pet me;" pinching my nose when I said, "Oink, oink," etc.). He was clearly able to find the appropriate parts of the body on the pictures.

Individual recognition of certain photographs, which was not at all clear in P (7:15) or L (9 months), became very plain in P (9:22) and L (9:8). These were photographs of their mother and of me. They were quite small and had been taken long ago. During this same period, playing with dolls began. *Spontaneous* acts indicating identification of the doll with a human being were now apparent.

Thus L (9 months) held her doll over the potty with an obvious purpose in mind (a very imperfect adaptation in its detailed execution since she held the doll upside down). The first indication of jealousy of the doll appeared when their mother pretended to fondle it (L, 7 months; P, 8 months).

During the last three months of the first year, indications of interest in pictures increased. The children contemplated photographs at length and tried to comb the hair of a woman in a portrait. When asked to do so, they would execute such acts as touching the hand or the foot in a picture or attempting to eat painted candy. The figure of a child on a black bronze clock was perfectly familiar to both children when they were ten months old. Finally, the most remarkable evidence of progress in abstract thought was that a very rough drawing I had made with a few strokes of the pencil was immediately recognized by P (9:17) and by L (9:8). Repeated testing by means of the games mentioned above yielded the same results.

Instead of attempting to ascertain whether an infant can recognize pictures of human beings when they are shown to him, we might ask ourselves whether an infant imagines the invisible parts of the body and is able to situate them in their proper places. Here are a few facts. The arm of L's doll had fallen off; *a few days afterward,* I gave it to L, asking her to put it back on. She placed it fairly accurately across the doll's chest (a little too low; 1 year). At 11:10 she tried to put her own shoes on her doll, hesitating about whether to place them on its head or feet, but she wound her stockings around the doll's legs. At 11:20 P looked for the breast in other people of both sexes and identified the proper place accurately. In all these acts something more than habits relating to individual objects is involved. A general notion of shapes and positions emerges from these special perceptions.

Let us go one step further. Will an infant associate parts of the human body with the corresponding parts of animals' bodies? There is no reason to believe that he will during the sixth and seventh months. But at 11:20 P seemed to be able to identify certain parts of the body of a wooden horse that had been given to him. He touched its eyes and stared at them attentively; he kissed its head and, in response to a request, tried to make it say *brr*. At one year and eight days he recognized the nose of a red rubber lamb (*oink-oink*). At 12:4 he kissed the head of birds carved in relief on a piece of furniture and made the *brr* sound. When L was one year old, she spintaneously pointed to a highly stylized ornamental detail on a white curtain, whose existence I would never have thought she would notice, calling it *dada*.

These associations do not imply that an infant is fooled by resemblances. He also notices differences. Although assimilation is at times spontaneous, at other times it is present only if stimulated. We ask an infant to seek an analogy and he discovers it. P puts hairpins in my hair because he has been asked to "take them to Papa," without receiving any indications as to precisely where to put them. He takes the red point of my elbow for a nipple ("*nénin*"); this was one of the first words uttered; he used it spontaneously but made no attempt whatsoever to suck my elbow. His attitude toward dolls, even those that are the size of an infant, shows that he differentiates between them and infants. Perception of a similarity is expressed by a partial transference of reaction from one object to another,

whereas perception of an identical object implies a total transference.

Such progress in the domain of abstract thought shows that
we are no longer dealing with simple, particular mental images
but with actual objective *notions* about the human body and
its parts. But these notions in their finished form apply to the
infant's own body just as they do to the body of his counter-
parts; they are at once objective and subjective. I have already
indicated the difficulties this last stage involves. The manner
in which an infant acquires knowledge of his own body and
its movements is quite different from the way in which he learns
about the bodies of others. The reason for this is that the sensations he experienced originally have no counterpart in external
knowledge (if we except the very limited parts of himself which
we have termed the *object* parts of the body). What sort of an
idea does he have of himself? How does conscious awareness of
self and of others take shape?

II

The Level of Experience. Psychologists have often traced the
gradual development of self-awareness. Through the phenomenon of twofold contact, touch enables the individual to make
an initial distinction between physical self and external things.
The kinesthetic sensation differentiates between one's own
movements and those of external objects. My body is an object
that is continuously present, given, whereas other bodies appear
and disappear. An infant presumably notices this and thus establishes some sort of order amid the chaos of his primitive perceptions. But doesn't this make an infant appear to be a creature
avid for pure knowledge and objective classifications? Just as
Buffon's first man suddenly awakens from nothingness to em-
brace philosophical thought, so "the infant of traditional psychology" immediately discovers these classifications, which he
will have some difficulty understanding twenty years later. Have
we the right to think of such knowledge as independent of the

needs to which it responds? It is not enough to maintain that certain classifications are *possible*; we must show that they are real, and what the motive is that leads to such analysis. The same question not only concerns means, it also arises in regard to ends. To what needs, to what habits, does the conflict between the self and the nonself correspond?

Difficulties Relating to the Theories of Self-Awareness. Scholars have managed to support the following two theses with conviction: the infant is involved first of all with his affective sensations; the infant's attention is drawn to the external world, to objects. The two theses will be recognized as not at all contradictory if we do not lose sight of the fact that before an object and its special attributes are distinguished, only qualified experiences or objects exist (in relation to instincts or habits). The infant's attention is attracted to the object solely because of the object's relation to an individual who is himself not part of the picture.

To speak of the chaotic impressions of the newborn infant, among which order is established only very gradually, is to forget that the infant is an organized being whose sensory excitations persist in conscious awareness only if they involve some constituted function. Nothing is more misleading than this portrayal of chaos. Indifferent to time and space, lacking memories that provide a basis for comparison, shut off from most sources of the interest that things have for adults, the infant appears to us mainly as a limited and yet perfectly balanced consciousness in which there is always harmony between perception and action.

It is quite impossible that a conflict should exist between the subject and the object early in the life of an infant. Likewise out of the question is any conflict between the sensory quality characteristic of things and the affective quality characteristic of the personal reaction of the subject to these things. For an infant there exist only things — more or less familiar, interesting, good or bad, friendly or hostile. The distinction between the thing in itself and its significance to me is abstract and comes later. The thing and our attitude or action in regard to it constitute an inseparable whole. The only differences that matter are not those that exist between the subject and the object but rather those that prevail between various qualified objects.

Subjectivity, the relation to the self of certain qualities attributed to objects, is not an infant's idea, nor even that of most men, but a belated product of psychological analysis. In order to possess it, we must first conquer our habits and even our repulsions. We tell ourselves that this thing is good or beautiful, not that this thing is good or beautiful for us. The value of the thing consists in the effect it has on my organism or on my mind because of its own nature. My impressions, my sensations, my states of consciousness — these are abstract ideas that are completely foreign to an infant. Only when we study the philosophers do we come to consider a thing good or beautiful, as a kind of binary composite: the thing, on the one hand, and its quality or value on the other; that is to say, sensations and sentiments. It is the idealist who teaches us to see in the thing itself a mere complex of sensations, and who demonstrates that we know only ourselves, love only ourselves.

The Notion of the Person. Therefore a *virtual self*, constituted by all that analysis, stripping the thing of some of its attributes, will one day classify as the subject. Meanwhile, for the infant there are only qualified objects or experiences. It is consequently probable that in the beginning the parts of his body that he can perceive are not essentially distinct from other things. They are merely objects close to him, and familiar. The question is merely one of degree. The sensitivity that characterizes the parts of his body does not serve as a basis for sufficient differentiation. The infant's attention is not focused on general or special sensitivity as a source of information about the body. It is the properties of his body far more than his organs or its mechanisms that interest him. It takes a great deal of observation to be able to exclude from direct awareness such things as clothing and familiar objects. The infant feels that someone is touching his clothing, his hair, or his hand, but he can no more locate the touch than a blind man with the end of his cane. He turns his head to see better the object he indirectly perceived or heard. He moves his hand toward it, etc. But this does not prove that he attributes to his body or to his sensory organs the role of intermediary. He is unaware of its function but makes use of it mechanically. Affective sensations are more characteristic of the self. At first, pain is belatedly recognized as a sensory property relating to *all* parts of the body. For us, of course, pain is not a property of the object in the same sense as is its color or warmth, but this kind of differentiation occurs much later. Isn't it true that pain, whether stemming from within us or from external causes, is a kind of troublesome or harmful object which inefficient reflexes attempt to dissipate? Nor does a sensation such as effort, which in the psychology of Maine de Biran constitutes the point of departure for self-awareness, possess this special attribute. For example, we associate with a heavy object the sensations we experience in our efforts to move it. Later, such confusion will be eliminated through reflection, but the problem is irrelevant at the early stage in an infant's development with which we are concerned.

Should we conclude that our body seems to us a special object over which our will exerts an immediate influence, whereas other objects are only moved through the intervention of our limbs? Yet the infant is no more aware of his will than he is of his sensitivity. At this point let me remind the reader that the desire to move one's body is not always efficient. If it does become efficient, the factor responsible therefor is often the intervention of other people. Moreover, the same characteristics are present in the infant's desire to move objects. Even later, after he has acquired mastery over his movements, what attracts his attention is the effect rather than the means. His gaze is riveted on the movement of the coveted body and not on that of his hands or legs, which, because of the reflexes called into play by the sight of the object, execute movements of which he is unaware.

It is probably an exaggeration to say that the infant, whose attention is monopolized by the external world, never notices his body and his limbs. Knowledge of his body, although it is quite partial and incomplete, exists at a very early age. But there is no reason to believe that he makes any significant distinction between his body and all the rest. An infant playing with his foot seems to behave toward it as he would toward any foreign object. Later it will become a familiar object, like his hand. *Mine*, as William James has demonstrated, is certainly a concept that develops after *me*. *Me* gradually becomes the most important, the most interesting part of things, somewhat like a second-degree *mine*. Although the infant is less and less inclined to treat one of his limbs as a vague object, the same is also true of his attitude toward his mother, his bottle, his toys. The distinction here is merely one of interest and quality. No actual *conflict* between "me" and "not-me" exists as yet.

Baldwin's Theory. Let us therefore begin with the hypothesis that the infant at first knows only *qualified objects*, among which the parts of his body do not as yet stand out as clearly as they subsequently will. Nowhere do we find in the infant the seed of a conscious conflict between the subject and the object. But although it is true that an idea exists only by virtue of imitation, through conflict with other ideas, the first form of the notion of self in an infant's consciousness is not that of the "me" as distinguished from the "not-me" but of the "me" as distinguished from all other persons.

As we have seen, the human being very quickly and clearly stands out from the uniform background of things, not because of his projection of the subject's attributes — the subject is not yet aware of himself — but because for the infant man is the most useful, the most interesting of all objects, owing to his constant connection with the infant's vital functions. In tracing the history of the notion of the individual, Baldwin (1) distinguishes four phases:

1) The ability to perceive mobile objects, the principal agents of an infant's pleasures and pains. The person who rocks him, dresses him, and fondles him is only a "collection of movements."

2) People are distinct from other objects because of the relatively capricious nature of their movements. Their behavior, which the infant attempts to anticipate and whose features he studies with fascination, remains to some extent enigmatic and unpredictable. People constitute a collection of totally unstable experiences.

3) However, this incoherence is only relative. The infant finally manages to detect individual characteristics. His attitude varies, depending on the person.

These three preliminary stages belong to the projective or objective phase of notions about an individual. In my opinion, Baldwin overemphasizes the difference between the chaotic activity of people and the rigorous determinism of things. The infant is almost totally unaware of this determinism. Much more important is the idea Baldwin seemed to stress in the beginning — the notion of a difference in interest. Soon this interest is linked to perception of the human form, a process whose evolution we have examined. In dealing with this process, as well as with that of distinguishing the subject from the object, it is well to remain somewhat leery of intellectualist illusions.

4) Here the second phase begins. Subjective elements that stem from the infant's organic sensations and emotions will now be added to the projective elements provided by the perception of others. Baldwin underscores the role of imitation, which he views as a bridge between these two kinds of elements:

But it is only when peculiar experience arises which we call effort that there comes that great line of cleavage in his experience which indicates the rise of volition, and which separates off the series now first really *subjective*. What has formerly been "projective" now becomes "*subjective*." This we may call the *subjective* stage in the growth of the self-notion. It rapidly assimilates to itself all the other elements by which the child's own body differs in his experience from other active bodies — all the passive inner series of pains, pleasures, strains, etc. Again it is easy to see what now happens. The child's subject sense goes out by a sort of return dialectic to illuminate the other persons. The "project" of the earlier period is now lighted up, claimed, clothed with the raiment of selfhood, by analogy with the subjective. The subjective becomes *ejective*; that is, other people's bodies, says the child to himself, have experiences *in them* such as mine has. They are also *me*'s; let them be assimilated to my me-copy. This is the third stage; the ejective, or social self, is born.

The "ego" and the "alter" are thus born together. Both are crude and unreflective, largely organic. And the two get purified and clarified together by this twofold reaction between project and subject, and between subject and eject. My sense of myself grows by imitation of you, and my sense of yourself grows in terms of my sense of myself. Both *ego* and *alter* are thus essentially social; each is a *socius* and each is an imitative creation.[2]

The Social Elements Involved in the Self-Image. It is important to indicate exactly what I think about the thesis of this American psychologist. Baldwin (2) was struck by the fact that the notion of others comprises a great variety of projective elements, only some of which are gradually assimilated by the subject. Other people are continually presenting new models to imitate. Our personality is enriched by the process of learning to imitate. On the other hand, to acts executed by others we give back the subjective quality they assumed in our imitation. Although the notion of an aptitude I acquired by imitation is due to others who serve as models, why will a trace of its social origin remain in my thoughts afterward? To take the very example Baldwin cites, if I learn to ride a bicycle *like my friend W*, initially I see this new aspect of myself only through the example set by my friend. But after I have mastered the feat completely, why should the idea of the *alter* persist? Why — to use Baldwin's language — should the self that has acquired a habit preserve

2. James Mark Baldwin, *Social and Ethical Interpretations in Mental Development: A Study in Social Psychology* (New York: Macmillan Co., 1899), pp. 8–9.

such a strong imprint, such an ever present memory of the self
in the process of adaptation?

Inner Thoughts and Imitation. The situation is not quite the
same if we accept the idea I have attempted to demonstrate:
the perception the infant has of himself gives him only frag-
mentary elements of a mental image of his own person. This
image is, in large part, an indirect consequence of imitation,
and it can be constructed only with elements provided by the
perception of the imitated models. If I no longer remember these
models individually, the image that I now form of my own
activity, insofar as it is not only felt but *pictured,* externalized,
still preserves features of the *alter*'s image, to which it owes its
origin. Baldwin seems to believe that a direct perception of the
similarity of organs and movements forms the basis of the two
notions: the self and the other. But this is a vast exaggeration.
The objective nucleus of the notion of self is very slight. The
subjective impressions which accompany the activity still cling
to objects. At first the infant has no *conception* of self. He does
not compare himself with others as an entity. The effects of
imitation alone serve to eradicate his unconscious egocentricity.

The infant has no conscious internal life. He is not aware
of the tendencies awakened in him by the individual or the
object. His impressions are merely a part of things, in the same
way as are their objective characteristics. All the affective exten-
sions of a human being's perception, all its reverberations in
the sphere of emotions and desires, remain inherent in their
sensory aspect.

Consequently, there is never a moment in the life of an infant
when he discovers his similarity to other beings, in the sense in
which this might imply that he combines the notion of the
subjective self with that of external man as he observes him.
Before he is able to imitate or speak, the infant does not think
of himself; he thinks of what interests him — which is something
quite different. "Internal states of mind" could become the object of thought only if for the infant there were *several* subjects

of which these states of mind would represent a manner of being. The *me* is unaware of itself as long as it is the universal subject, the center of the world. To think, it is said, is to classify, to assimilate. But how can one think about a unique subject, an incomparable being around whom *everything* is ordained and from whom *everything* derives its true value? The egocentricity of the infant is such a profoundly natural phenomenon that it can only be unconscious at first. It is imitation that gradually causes the self to emerge from the unconscious. The first conscious *idea* will not be that of the self, center of the universe (which psychological analysis will later affect), but on the contrary the notion of an objective self. This objective self is but one unity like all others, since the infant imitates others and achieves self-awareness in so doing. This is the beginning of the social being, the unity of the human or animal family. This *idea* is in constant conflict with impulses that stem from the unconscious egocentric domain, and the infant's learning process as well as man's ethical and social life are both aspects of this conflict.

Would an infant who grew up alone (if such a thing were possible) have a notion of self? This seems doubtful. Perhaps the self would remain unconscious, virtual, intimately connected with things, in the absence of an objective image which, because of the special attention it arouses, would serve as a prop for the mental image. In such a being, the image of the world would resemble a picture in which everything speaks to an invisible spectator in relation to whom the perspective would be regulated. Can we assume that the spectator would finally appear to himself, as in those old cavalry maps where the artist naively painted himself in the foreground as he was making his sketch, as if the point of view could be seen? Be that as it may, under real circumstances this kind of personality splitting is not necessary.

Other people give us an objective image that helps us to make the transition from what is experienced to what is represented.

But not all the modes of the infant's and other people's relations are of a nature to foster the infant's self-awareness. The person who cares for him, and from whom he fears or hopes to receive the kind of treatment consonant with his needs, at first appears to him in a way that excludes any reciprocity, any assimilation. All this changes when imitation begins. If we were to single out particular phases in the evolution of self-awareness, it would be those we examined when dealing with the development of imitation itself. First comes the identity of the objective effects obtained, the immediate objects of interest (voice emission, movement of objects). Marking as it does the beginning of the initial analogous self-image, it can be mirrored in the person of another because it achieves the same results. The notion then grows more precise as the triple transfer of *motor power*, *affective value*, and *attention* takes place, proceeding from the object to the individual model, with all his attitudes and gestures. We are not reduced here to any arbitrary suppositions about the classifications the infant will establish. Imitation, and all the feelings that accompany it (sympathy, emulation, envy, jealousy) and that will emerge suddenly in the infant's attitude and behavior, are the objective marks of the (hidden) intellectual phenomenon. They enable us to record the date when imitation begins and to follow its progress thereafter.

Moreover, and this is what Baldwin analyzed in such a masterly fashion, it is always imitation that much later reveals to each of us new aspects of the self, that makes us aware of the uneven evolution of this complex knowledge.

I have found a charming expression of this idea in a note by J. Paulhan (47) on the interpretation of certain dreams. When and how do we become aware that certain ideas are really our own? As long as they are not obvious to us, they do not seem to be our very own. We become aware of them by assuming that they have become foreign to us and that we are seeing them propounded by *someone else*. "What would I say if *someone* came to me and claimed that. . . ?" The lecturer wonders what effect he is having on his listeners and puts himself in their place in order to judge himself as someone else would judge him. I will quote the conclusion of this note: "All the ideas about self which we form in this way probably signify that we are, despite appearances, men like other men. . . . We are formed by men perhaps because we live mainly among men. The idea of self is a little like that of the bat in La Fontaine's fable — a very sincere bat who takes himself for a rat when he visits rats and for a bird when he falls into a bird's nest." Probably we should add the following reservation: to the extent that the bat knows how to imitate. Imitation, the principle of assimilation, determines the limits of assimilation even as it perfects it.

III

Objective Language. Language is the most delicate expression of intellectual phenomena. We may seek in it the confirmation of our thesis.

The infant's first words can hardly be classified in grammatical terms. For example, P's first words (toward the end of the first year) are used for purposes that may be called indicative and imperative, intellectual and affective. *Papa, mama,* at times express the desire to be taken in our arms or to be given some specific attention; at others they merely signify a recognition of our presence or that of an object that is associated specifically with us (for instance, my empty chair in my study). *A plus* (no more, in baby talk) is repeated during that period to signify a statement of fact; when, for example, we tell him that there is no more candy. But it also expresses his personal will when he refuses to drink his milk or eat his soup, or when he resists our efforts to dress him. *Tata* is used to announce his need to go to the toilet, but he also says it when he sees soiled clothes (a statement or explanation). Probably the first meaning is used more frequently in the beginning. But both appear more or less at the same time. This should not surprise us if we remember that spoken language postdates understood language and constitutes only a small part of it. An infant's spoken language frequently refers to his needs and desires. On the other hand, it often represents an invitation to perceive, to notice a fact or a quality.

Thus, the words uttered designate both objects and facts, as well as the subjective feelings and desires that accompany them. But, in reference to the latter, what subjective feelings are involved? Those of the infant himself or those of other people? Let us call the first *subjective* and the second *objective*. The subjective meaning is perhaps the primitive one, probably because we speak to the infant or in his presence far more about things that momentarily interest him than we do about the feelings and needs of other people. But we shall see that very quickly the two meanings become interdependent. In the first months of the second year the infant moves with ease from one to the other. Assimilation is thus either about to be achieved or already has been achieved.

Examples. We notice this first of all in regard to the parts of the body. *Main-main* (hand) was used by L (9:15) either to ask someone to shake her hand or to express recognition of a hand seen in a photograph. When we said "hand" or "foot" to her brother (12:25), he would point to his own hand or foot as well as to someone else's. Later (18 months), he would do the same in response to such words as mouth, tooth, eye, or head. Actually, as early as 11:14, words that denoted games but that also referred to certain parts of the body (nose, mouth, ear) were understood to mean both the infant's and someone else's nose, mouth, or ear.

The same is true of acts. For some time P (15 months) used the expression *pipi* to mean urinate. He said *pipi* quite spontaneously when he saw a little girl's underclothes being lifted. His sister (12:18) used the same word when she noticed the dishwater draining on the rack. *Nénin*, hitherto used to express a desire to be nursed, was now uttered spontaneously in an interrogatory tone (Do you want to be nursed?), or as an order to his mother to nurse a baby who was crying (P, 15 months).

A special characteristic of a verb is, of course, that it can be conjugated — in other words, that it applies to the acts of both the subject and others. P (15 months) already understood this twofold character of such verbs as to go to bed, to sleep, to dress, to button, etc. In the case of spoken language, *kir* (*écrire*) meant "I want to write"; but P also said, "*Papa kir*" (Papa is writing — 16:25).

One would think that certain words would retain a purely subjective meaning for a long time — words that express pleasure, pain, desire, or will. Nothing of the kind is true. P (14:3) said *bobo* when he hurt himself. He used it in referring to a slight injury to his eye as well as to a crease in his sock which caused some discomfort in his foot. But he likewise used it in alluding to his doll's broken leg. He said, "*Mama bobo*" upon noticing a blister on his mother's lip (15:18), and also when he perceived a chair that seemed to be broken (14:25). In his presence we mentioned someone whose feet were hurting. He said "*bobo*," pointing to *his* foot. In addition, he used the word to convey the idea of scolding or hitting. When he saw a very small infant crying, he muttered "*peur-bobo*." *Peur* (fear) is a word he used both subjectively and objectively (15 months). As for L, (1 year), she used the word *dodo* to express a desire to go to sleep, but she also uttered it when she put her doll to sleep or when she saw her brother in bed. She said *pam!* not only when she herself fell down but also when she saw an object or a person fall.

Perhaps we have not been mindful enough that what we have been pointing out here likewise applies to all words. Is there a verbal term for purely internal psychic data? A totally subjective word would be useless. Words can only serve to identify those realities of which everyone is aware; they correspond to notions of which certain elements at least must be objective. The word for an emotion such as fear, for example, is of no practical value unless I can say, in quite determinate circumstances, not only "I am afraid" but also "he is afraid."

As far as infantile language is concerned, we might ask ourselves whether this duality — the fact of being both objective and subjective — is a result or a cause of the assimilation of the self and of others. The mental development of the infant proceeds in accordance with a complicated causality. Doubtless language is at once both cause and effect. The meaning of an expression depends not only on the manner in which it is said by the infant's familiars but also on the mental effort made by the infant himself, beginning with the employment of the same word to designate two different but similar objects. The infant uses this word either because he hears both of the objects referred to in this way or because he personally perceives the similarity. In the first case, the infant's attention will be attracted by the identity of the term to a similarity that he might otherwise not have noticed. It is quite true that the word used for one particular part of the body can serve as a link between the object and the subject. The singularity of the word would antedate that of the idea. But one must not exaggerate the influence of the word. Like the influence of the educative processes employed in an environment that is responsive to the infant's gestures, the influence of the word accelerates the formation of habits; but it is not an essential precondition of this formation, at least so far as common-sense notions are concerned. I therefore believe that in principle the twofold use of words constitutes primarily an effect of interdependence which has already been established between the subjective and objective elements of the notion. If this were not so, the assimilation of current language would prove an insurmountable obstacle for an infant. Our experiments show not even a trace of such difficulty, because imitation has already lent subjective significance to all the perceptions of a human being.

The Proper Name. We will understand the relationship between imitation and self-awareness even better if we examine the use of the infant's proper name and its substitutes.

In the initial phase which for P began around 3:15, his name was at first merely a device for attracting his attention. He turned his head when he heard his name being called (specialized form of the reaction of attention to sound). The sound of a human voice, its intonation together with the articulation of a particular proper name, became a cue for an invitation to participate in interesting "experiences," that is, in something or other that was related to the infant's instinctive tendencies.

By the end of the first year the infant's name had come to be an invitation for him to direct his activities, which until then were directed toward others, toward himself instead. Thus P, when a year old, would brush both his mother's stockings and mine in response to a request from me. Then I would say to him: "Brush P's stockings." After some hesitation on his part and repeated injunctions from me, the act I requested was finally performed.

In this experiment no indicative gesture was made by me; not even a passive direction was given. The experiment succeeded solely because of the prior use of such procedures. Similarly, P's sister, when she was a year old, performed on her own person acts she was accustomed to performing on others (pinching her nose with her fingers, etc.). She did this when we spoke her name and asked her. She hesitated somewhat about the exact localization of the gesture but had no difficulty whatsoever about its general direction, whether the act was performed on herself or on others. The proper name, then, became the cue for an increasingly extended series of acts performed by the infant on his own person, in contrast to similar acts executed on others.

One such act performed by the infant consisted in pointing to the person named. First, the infant learned to point to others. P (1 year) could point to papa and mama (looking in the direction of the person named had occurred long before). But he was nonplussed when asked, "Where is P?" When we compare this experiment with the preceding one, we will see that the system of reactions stimulated by the proper name (closely interdependent later) develops very gradually.

During the first months of the second year both children became familiar with the names of a good many people they knew. They pronounced these names quite spontaneously. But not until the sixteenth month did they utter their own names for the first time. And even then it occurred in an artificial manner. We had taught them to answer the question, "What's your name?" It is more interesting to note, in the first spontaneous verbal combinations, how long it took the infant to pronounce his own name once he had learned to articulate the names of others. Generally, at the outset, no subject or personal predicate is given utterance. When the infant first learns the names of others, he continues for several months to repeat them without at any time naming himself.

Thus although *kir* signifies I want to write or I am writing, L (16:25) will readily say "*papa kir*" (I want papa to write, or papa is writing). In actuality, the proper name is pronounced only in response to explicit or implicit questions such as: Who? To whom? For whom? This is a matter of ascertaining whether P or his friend will receive a cookie; or when P wants to do himself what he saw someone else do: in other words, when he wants to *imitate*. It is through the contrast between self and the others that the idea of self becomes objectified. But this contrast implies a kind of assimilation. The conscious self has fallen from that privileged place that belongs to the latent self. When an idea is presented without specifying the subject or personal object, it is this latent self that is being expressed. "To write" represents a certain interesting, indecomposable experience. "Paul writes" implies a special attentive emphasis on the person who writes; this is *substituted* for papa, who is holding the pen, in order to enable the infant to play an identical role, to *imitate*. This is no longer an "experience" but a *notion* in which the basic similarity of the author of one and the same action becomes confirmed.

The Pronoun. Certain common names or pronouns can be substituted for proper names. When P began to name himself, he also used the expression *nini*, which at times meant himself and at others signified some other child. The self became individualized as an object of thought, but only insofar as it constituted a singular human entity (18 months).

A little later the personal pronoun appeared. The accidental use of words such *I* or *me* in certain isolated phrases does not in itself imply the idea of a *me* as a product of assimilation, such as we understand it. These expressions can be simple substitutes for gestures or attitudes, mere volitional interjections (Give me! or, I want some!). Characteristic of the idea of self are the complex reactions which such isolated uses of the words presuppose; the same is true for the correct interpretation of these words when others utter them. This manner of handling an interchangeable verbal tool, as well as its relative rather than absolute use, is a sign that the infant's unconscious egocentricity is on the wane.

When P was about nineteen months old, the personal pronoun made its appearance: "Me!" (In answer to such questions as: Who? To whom? For whom?). He spoke the word in order to be given an object he saw in someone else's hands. Soon this was followed by "you" (to urge someone to imitate an act he had just performed). Other words expressed the increasingly apparent awareness of the identity of the subject and of other members of the social group. For example, the child would say about one of his imitative games: "To André! to Paul!" (himself) "to everyone" (20 months). The same period witnessed the appearance of comparative terms such as the word *like* (like papa).

Thus the child initially identifies himself by pronouncing his own name and referring to himself in the third person. Next the pronoun *I* or *me* appears. At eighteen months this occurs rarely; but after a lapse of a few months it reappears and toward the end of the second year becomes a regular occurrence in the wake of a certain amount of difficulty with the proper name. Whereas a person's name has a fixed attribute, the pronoun designates either whichever person is speaking or the person to whom one is speaking. The child who says *I* in alluding to himself knows that others allude to themselves in the same way. This involves a further step in the assimilation of the person who is the subject and the person who is the object. I would like to connect this kind of grammatical progress to an anecdote of that period which seems to symbolize the sort of evolution that is taking place. I put the military jacket I was wearing on P. He ran around the room marching and shouting: "Papa! One! Two!" The pronoun is somewhat like the jacket that was passed from one person to another, in accordance with the role played by each individual. The function becomes more important than the individual who performs it. Thanks to the process of imitation, the seeds of the social personality are thus always sown.

Attitudes of Assimilation. We must relate this progress of assimilation in language to a whole series of interesting acts: those in which the child treats other people as they themselves treat him — that is, as a child. He usually imitates the treatment given to *another* child. Later and more rarely, he imitates acts that he can only see performed in relation to himself. I shall not in this connection stress the early attitudes of both children toward their dolls. They were obviously acquired or suggested as a consequence of the manner in which they saw dolls treated by other children when they went to the park. But the following are authentic examples of imitation: P played with a little ten-month-old girl (14:20) and taught her games that he had been taught earlier. L (14:15) gave her doll a sheet of paper and held the doll so that it could lean against it. She suggested that the doll "write." (She said *técrire* instead of *écrire.*) She accused the doll of having wet her bed (22 months) and attributed responses to the doll which she herself was making. She spoke to the doll the way we spoke to her (23 months): "Touch the night light and burn yourself!" Even toward her mother she assumed a maternal, protective attitude. She put her arm around her mother's neck, consoled her, reassured her by saying: "Don't be afraid, dolly. You're my little girl. Don't cry. I'll take you with me," etc. Generally speaking, the child's attitude toward his parents is dominated by unconscious habits. This reversal of roles attests the development of *notions* about these roles. At first the "me" becomes objectified in the person of other children, dolls, etc., and is treated like other "me's." Then the imagination is satisfied with the use of a simple symbol. The parents, stripped of their own personal characteristics, become the concrete prop for the child's idea. Here, not only the "me" as *agent* becomes objectified but also the "me" as *patient*. The child no longer visualizes only what he can do; he also imagines the kinds of treatment of which he may be the object. In some way the latter is seen from the outside and no longer felt from within. The attitude the child is imitating is an element in a scenario in which two persons are the actors. Each plays his role only because he has a partner that is more or less transfigured by imagination.

This kind of imitation, as the dates of the example indicate, necessarily occurs later. The most difficult thing for a young child to imitate is the manner in which other people behave toward him, assuming that he is the *only* person to whom such attentions are being addressed. Thus the forms of language that the child hears spoken to others — at least when they have become entirely familiar to him — are imitated more easily than those used when people speak to him. For example, during L's initial years my wife and I never used the familiar form, *tu*, in remarks addressed to her, whereas she heard it used when we addressed her brother and when we spoke to each other. Yet she always and unhesitatingly used the familiar form in speaking to us. The formal *vous* was nonetheless not unfamiliar to her. Thus, she repeated after her brother, jokingly (22:14), "*Monsieur vous avez. . . .*" In three other instances which I noted during her twenty-third month, L said to the maid: "*D, donnez le café. . . . D, ne touchez pas. . . . D, vous avez vu.*" Each time the formal rather than the familiar form was used (L was not repeating anything she had just heard). This showed that she could use the formal form — although she did not do so regularly — when she spoke to someone who in her hearing had always been addressed in this way. But in her own manner of speaking there was no imitation whatsoever of the way in which *she herself* was invariably addressed by all the people around her.

To summarize: What, then are the components of the child's developing awareness of his similarity to others? To say that the object is to ascertain how the individual comes to incorporate within the body of his fellowmen a soul similar to his own is to state the problem poorly; yet this is how it was posed in the past. The real point of departure is the infant's unconscious egocentricity, which can be defined only as a negation of the categories of reflective thought. Through imitation, the infant's vital feelings become objectified and the image of his own physical and psychic person is constructed, patterned after the image of others and reacting on this image. The development of speech enables us to mark out the various stages in this assimilation: the employment of subjective words in alluding to oneself and to others; the naming of acts, organs, and physiological states; the use of verbs expressing functions common to both the subject and his models; the use of the proper name, which then becomes a possible subject for these verbs; the use of the pronoun, which stresses the identity of the function. Awareness of oneself as a human being is a collective term for this indefinite category of actions which gradually becomes enriched in the course of psychic evolution.

Similarity and Contiguity. The thesis I have just expounded is open to a theoretical objection; discussion of this objection will enable me to offer a better definition of my postulates.

If assimilation results from acts which, in the beginning, are not necessarily characteristic of conscious imitation, how do such acts acquire the characteristics in question? We have said that the sense of similarity stems first from objective results obtained by the child and that he compares these results to those obtained by the model, since he perceives them in the same way. We readily concede that the feeling of similarity can be easily extended to those parts of the body we call *objects* (the hands, the foot, etc.). We have demonstrated the power that exists in the child's mind so far as the objective assimilation of forms is concerned. It is not at all surprising that he should assimilate his hand with the hand of the model, since he can recognize this part of the body even when it is sketched very roughly (one year). But we have also shown that this process has its limitations. It is thus true that assimilation, the objective imitation established between most of the movements and attitudes of both the model and the child, cannot be based on anything other than the relations of *contiguity*, whatever they might be, between a habitual reaction and an ordinary cue. This being so, how can assimilation appear to be similar to the relationships of resemblance?

It is doubtless because of their interdependence with the visible, objective aspects of the act that the invisible aspects themselves are connected to the corresponding aspects of the model's act. The child *notices* that the sounds he utters are similar to those uttered by someone else. Isn't it natural for him to *believe* that the invisible movement of his own lips resembles the movement of the model's lips? And wouldn't he even have the illusion of *feeling* this similarity directly? So inevitable is this illusion that nothing can belie it, since the child can have no direct visual perception of the movement of his own lips that might hinder assimilation.

But we must go even further. The problem considered here does not arise exclusively in connection with imitation. A good many metaphors are based on associations through contiguity, although in the end they create a confused picture of the similarity between objects. Such metaphors combine two categories of heterogeneous sensations. Musical sounds seem *high* or *low* to us because the larynx rises or falls; much depends on whether the sounds are sharp or flat, whether they seem to us to be at different levels of the instrument of emission (head voice or chest voice, etc.). We believe, however, that we can perceive some sort of inherent affinity between high and low sounds. The resemblance resides not in the direction from which sound emanates nor in the sounds themselves but rather in the spatial distance between these directions and the complex phenomenon of voice emission in the human larynx. Similarly, psychological language abounds in metaphors ranging "from the physical to the psychic." Actually, there is no resemblance between the physical and the psychic — this differentiation is meaningless — but only between complex, psychologically similar acts, one of which becomes intellectualized because it develops into something more significant than all the others. In both instances, however, the material and mental aspects can only be related through contiguity. Isn't the same thing true of imitation? The relationship of resemblance, as perceived by the subject, exists between the model's act, which is affected by sympathetic attention of a subjective value, and the subject's act, which is visualized in accordance with the objective characteristics of the model's act. Thus understood, resemblance exists solely between complex notions whose respective elements are united through contiguity — in other words, through initial imitations and the habits that result from them.

The Mirror Experiment. But, one might object, the child has many opportunities to form a direct visual image of almost all of his body and its movements. He has examined himself in a mirror, for example, and thus has a good idea of what he looks like externally — his physiognomy, his expressions. I do not believe that this is a negligible point. In *some* children this may accelerate the imitation of facial expressions and general attitudes; it may thus help to perfect self-awareness. But this is nonetheless accidental. Children who have never seen themselves in a mirror likewise engage in imitation and know themselves to be similar to other human beings.

Infants become interested very early in this familar image. They assume playful attitudes and make grimaces. I noticed this in P on several occasions toward the end of the third month and in L toward the end of the second. Let us describe in detail this learning process in L. First the infant stared without reacting. Then she recognized in the mirror objects or people that she also perceived alongside or behind her when she turned her head (influenced, for example, by tactile or auditory sensations, etc.). I noticed that at a certain point L (5:17) acquired the habit of turning around to see the real person whose image she had glimpsed in the mirror. A little later, photographs of people produced the same reaction: she turned around to look behind her for the original of the photo (9:20). In this case, the reaction, which she soon realized served no purpose, quickly ceased. Actually, the reaction of an infant who is looking into a mirror is confirmed, and it probably also becomes geometrically more precise: the apparent position of the image regulates the movement that is made to find the object. Finally, reactions occur whose point of departure is the infant's own image. The infant's movements, moreover, are associated through contiguity with the visual perception of movements that correspond to the image. In the end, the execution of the movement is controlled by a series of changes in the image which will even determine the initiative. Thus, the sight of a certain part of the image, which at first regulated the movement of the hand toward that particular part of the mirror, finally directs the hand movements toward the corresponding part of the body itself. For a while there is only the first reaction (normal reaction). Then the second reaction appears and becomes dominant (special reaction). In the beginning the infant tries to touch the mirror image, to kiss it, etc. Conversely, L (11:18), who since early morning had been wearing a straw hat to protect her head from possible falls, suddenly saw herself in the mirror. She quickly put her hand *to her head* to seize hold of this surprising object. We have often had occasion to verify this observation. Inversely, by the close of the second year, when L was dressed in a new coat, she ran to look at herself in the mirror.

Interpretation. Can we say that the infant *recognizes* himself in the mirror? To put it differently, how are we to interpret this facial expression? When the child looks into the mirror, his visual sensations determine new reactions which are directed toward the objects that occupy positions like those occupied by apparent objects. In particular, the person who is looking at himself has a reverse reaction. Finally, this image becomes a *familiar object* which tends, because of its very form (and not only because of its symmetrical position or its relationship to perceived changes), to determine these special reactions. It is the relationship of *contiguity*, not of similarity, that is established between the image and the self. The child can compare another person's image with the person himself, or his own image in the mirror with the images of other people, but he cannot compare himself with his image, since only through the image is he aware of himself as a visible form.

We must not hesitate to connect this exceptional mirror experiment with the experience of normal imitation. Other adults and also other children in the society in which he lives are for the infant the natural mirror that reflects for him his own image when he proceeds to imitate. In all these instances the infant simultaneously perceives his own gesture from within and that of the model or the image from without; at the same time he sees the link that connects the two, which is the result of contiguity.

One might argue that the infant *identifies himself* with his reflection in the mirror whereas he *compares himself* to others when he is imitating. Later he will say: "This is me, these are the others. I am acting *like* them." All this merely shows that one should not exaggerate the role of the relationship between the two. The contiguity of the subject's attitudes and of his image is constant and does not vary. The analogous relationship between the model and the subject is spasmodic and transitory. Yet the analogy is no less profound because of this.

Besides, one must not exaggerate the precision of the visual image of the body itself which results from this mirror perception. The very child who at 11:18 "recognized herself" so clearly in the mirror — in the sense in which we have used this expression — is not yet able six weeks later to perform directly on herself acts which she has performed without the slightest hesitation on others; pinching the nose, pulling the ear. For example, trying to pinch her own nose, she feels around, touches her cheek, then her upper lip beneath her nose. Finally she gives up trying to imitate. In the next few days she tries again and makes some progress. This kind of fumbling is all the more surprising because she had already played this game a few months earlier. But having learned it mechanically, she quickly forgot it, like everything else learned in this fashion.

If the *specific* image of the human body is still difficult to apply to oneself, there is all the more reason to believe that no precise *individual* image exists. The mirror image, if it is carefully studied, will finally lead to a more precise individual image. But for a long time the optic symmetry of the image and the individual and the similarity of their movements continue to be the prerequisites of recognition. Furthermore, the child recognizes himself no better in a picture. When P was one year old he recognized me in a snapshot but did not recognize himself as the baby in my arms.

I had taken a snapshot of a group of children. The next day I showed it to L, then two years and eight months old, who was included in the group. She immediately pointed to and named all the children in the group. But when she came to her own likeness she stopped short, nonplussed. I urged her to tell me who it was. She finally said: "A little girl." I asked her if she knew that little girl. "No," she answered. I told her the little girl was herself and I insisted that this was so. She seemed to accept my statement. The next day I tried again, but with the same result. Urged to name the little girl, she hesitated, then said: "It's M.R." (a little girl her own age). We can see, then, how very tenuous is the precise notion of one's own visual form, in spite of what the child learns from looking into a mirror.

In summary, awareness of our resemblance to others is not

the consequence of a direct comparison of visible forms. The point of departure is the similarity, in terms of imitation, of the effects of our acts. Imitation establishes an increasingly close interdependence between the subjective and objective aspects. From this, a *tendency* to construct an image of the self results. Only indirectly and a good deal later does the self-image become more precise.

V

The Problem of Constructive Imitation. Relationships of contiguity can then appear to be relationships of similarity. But our explanation is still incomplete. We must demonstrate how assimilation becomes both more precise and more limited. The sense of resemblance, which at first bears on the common objective elements of the two acts, is extended to include the interdependent elements of the initial act, which one feels differently in oneself than one does in others. Since this is so, why does the child not experience the illusion of a total similarity in the acts we have described? Actually, he employs *his own means* for the performance of these acts, in order to achieve a result similar to that achieved by the model. Generally speaking, how can imitation be perfected beyond the degree to which the objective, comparable result is achieved?

Let us state this caveat differently. We have for the most part studied the imitation of acts which the child already knows how to perform. Subordination of the perception of the model's movements has been added to acts that are already well defined in form. Whether the infant is proceeding on the basis of instinct, training, or trial and error, the purpose is to achieve an objective, *common* result. We still need to know how imitation can become the initiator of new acts whose very form is directly determined by the kind of imitation that functions as a cause.

If we could demonstrate that the sense of similarity first manifests itself by allowing many features of an act to remain indeterminate, the objection to our theory would instead become a confirmation.

In the beginning, the function of the act interests the infant far more than its form. If we put ourselves in the infant's place, we might have the impression that the process of imitation is taking place when we see a man doff his hat and a woman bow, or when he waves his hat and she waves her handkerchief. This is what happens to an infant when he uses his own personal means to imitate. Besides, his imitations are not confined to human beings alone. He imitates the sounds of animals and their movements; he even imitates objects, often through the intervention of a human being. And, unless I am mistaken, he does so rather late in his development. The child who imitates the engine of a train concentrates on certain things that lend themselves to imitation. He astonishes us as much by the boldness of his assimilations as by his indifference to what makes his imitation seem to us incoherent or ridiculous. One cannot say that these differences completely escape his notice; but they do not give him pause. His naive interpretation is quite unaffected by any of the misgivings or objections that would paralyze us.

A more precise sense of similarity does, however, gradually evolve. Imitation becomes less free and more accurate. It seems to me that this is due to the interactions of the imitated acts: sometimes the complex act is broken up into already familiar simple acts; sometimes several different acts comprise common features that free themselves from these acts by means of a species of abstraction. Thus, in the act of throwing a kiss, the model brings his hand to his mouth; this is a visible object, already familiar to the infant because of movements made in talking, eating, etc. Perception of the mouth is present as a common element in a certain number of habitually imitated acts. It develops in the course of time into an independent cue for all acts that are similarly localized. The notion of an organ or of a part of the body tends to evolve at the expense of all the acts with which this notion is concerned. In using the word notion, I mean to convey the point that the visual image of the object involved is henceforth penetrated by subjective elements common to the movements that the image determines in the child. Thus, every visible *detail* of the human body assumes a subjective significance. A system of increasingly precise relations is finally established through an analysis that tends to make each complex imitated act the focal point of many movements that are either *imitated or capable of being imitated.*

Obviously, this analysis makes possible not only syntheses but rectifications as well. When P saw me opening an umbrella, he tried at first to do likewise by pushing out the ribs. But on one occasion he watched my hand attentively as it moved along the handle toward the umbrella tip. Since the hand, because of prior acts, was a part of the body with which he was familiar, and inasmuch as a subjective significance had been added to his visual perception of it, he tried to imitate exactly what I did. His efforts proved vain at that stage because the power of analysis was not sufficiently developed to enable him to imitate the act of pressing the spring.

We are now in a position to understand the law governing the evolution of imitation. The suggestion of example initially stimulates an awakening of various familiar and more or less similar automatisms. This it does either through localization or through the form of the movement, depending upon which particular aspect attracted the child's attention. But in a child who has already acquired a certain number of imitative habits, the other aspects which more attentive observation (or better analysis of what he remembers) reveals to him also awaken motor tendencies that will be combined with the earlier habits. The correction results from an *organization* of earlier acts. There is connection here, which we can only indicate, between this evolution of imitation and the formation of new images. Involved at the start are systems of dissociated memories, the formation of new verbal combinations, and complex phrases imitated from daily speech in which the words gradually take on individual characteristics.

Syntheses and Corrections. It would be risky to attempt to re-constitute these syntheses. A few examples will suffice to show how difficult the problem is. P (1 year) imitated rather readily the gesture of threatening someone (you wait!). His right arm was horizontal, the forearm vertical, the hand spread over the cheek, the index finger raised, the other fingers bent. To explain all the features of this act, it is necessary to go back to its origins. The position of the arm and hand recalled earlier, now familiar acts learned passively. These included "Good-bye! Make a face! Dida! dida!" (pull your ear). The position of the index finger might be determined by certain earlier habits such as snapping one's fingers, writing, pointing at someone, making one's lips vibrate by rubbing a finger over them, rubbing one's gums with an index finger that has been dipped into teething syrup, etc. All these gestures were subordinated earlier to the sight of a similar gesture. Often the synthesis is not at first successful: the motor possibilities of the example are achieved successively or else they fail in a very unharmonious manner to materialize. For example, the child tries to imitate the little windmill game: the hands must turn around one another. The first attempts culminate in the reproduction of another game, that of banging with one's hands. Then P rubbed his hands (he was accustomed to washing his own hands), whereupon he was reminded of the game of the little puppets (rotation of the wrists, etc.). Such examples, admittedly inadequate, nonetheless show us how imitation becomes the formative factor in new complex modes of activity that give imitation its educative value. We must also realize that imitation as an inclusive category becomes more and more distinct from ordinary reactions in the infant's aware-ness. Responsible for this process is the intimate connection established between *elements* of the various acts.

It is primarily when new, artificial acts or simple gestures without any direct relationship to usual or useful movements are performed that the infant is unable, for a while at least, to execute precise imitation. In the beginning a distortion of the usual movement takes place because the infant's attention is attracted to something which has a somewhat farfetched similarity to the initial movement. Thus L (11:9) imitated the maid who was washing the floor. The gesture of her hands was correct, but instead of kneeling she was on all fours. She interpreted the gesture of spreading out her fingers or bringing them together by opening and closing her hand (13 months). Having seen in a store (14:15) an animated cardboard figure which oscillated with its head leaning sideways, while its eyes moved in the same direction, she imitated it a few moments later by turning her head toward the right and left (in other words, she interpreted rotation on a horizontal axis as rotation on a vertical one). The latter was much more familiar to her and was normally associated with lateral movements of the eyes. During the course of a series of tests in which the examples were very faithfully copied (22 months), she kneeled down on both her legs, leaning on her hand as she did so, instead of getting into this position by flexing both legs without leaning on anything, like the model. A little later, she copied walking on all fours by using her knees instead of her feet. She corrected herself after taking another look at the model. It was obvious that in this exercise, the starting position was imitated from an earlier, different one, the somersault. Thus she began by needlessly leaning the top of her head on the ground, which she had become accustomed to doing in the earlier exercise.

A general awareness of imitation was certainly present in both children by the end of the first year. This was evidenced by their requests to repeat certain attempts to imitate (for example, holding out an object so that an act can be performed and picking it up again for a second try). At eighteen months L asked if her imitation was correct ("Like that?") At twenty-two months she knew in advance what she could and could not do ("I don't know"). She pointed fairly quickly to the place on her own body that corresponded to the place I had pointed to on mine. I remarked to her that her doll had a hole in the top of its head. With a very accurate gesture she made sure that the same was not true of her own head (25 months). However, can you believe that after I had shown L how to find the thumb of one hand (2 years) and even though she could find the thumb of her other hand, she was unable to find my thumb? After several attempts, she managed to find it but only because I had placed my own hand directly next to hers! This confirms the point that *analysis* of even the most familiar perceptions develops quite slowly.

AFFECTIVE ASPECTS
OF
IMITATION

I

The Meaning of the Word Sympathy. In this chapter, the word sympathy should be understood in its etymological sense. That is, for the individual who experiences this feeling, it consists in an echo, a reverberation of a feeling that others have experienced. On the other hand, in its completely evolved, human form, it signifies awareness of the existence of feeling in others.

The very reality of this kind of sympathy presents a problem. The phenomenon appears more or less combined with others from which it can be isolated only with difficulty. Hence the ambiguity of the word, which has come to mean affection, kindness, active pity. The rush of anger, the gesture of reprisal or protection which the sight of a child being mistreated provokes in a man does not constitute sympathy in the sense that we attribute to the word. The fear aroused in another child who witnesses the spectacle comes much closer to the meaning we have in mind. We are tempted in this connection to isolate two different elements: sympathy, and immediately afterward the personal reactions of anger or helpfulness. However, this does not mean that the second is not, in certain cases, something primitive and therefore independent of the first. Some people see (and they are not wrong), a connection between sympathy and esthetic feeling, a sentiment that is free from these reactions, and yet rather far removed from infantile feelings.

In examining the phenomenon of sympathy, we might embark on the same path we followed when dealing with imitation. Isn't sympathy the affective aspect of imitation? The one involves the contagion of emotions; the other, the contagion of acts.

The Theory of Instinct. Let us examine first the thesis which maintains that sympathy is an instinct. Sociologists have often explained elementary forms of human sociability by the presence of both instinctive sympathy and instinctive imitation. This implies that the perception of phenomena expressing emotion engenders in the person who observes these phenomena a *corresponding emotional reflex.*

Such a thesis cannot fail to elicit the same reservations I expressed in regard to instinctive imitation. It is of course difficult to prove the existence of an instinct; yet it is even more difficult to prove that there is nothing instinctive in an affective or motor reaction. The analyses we shall present in the remainder of this chapter, however, may serve to invalidate the idea that the signs of emotion the child perceives provoke identical reactions in him.

A correct interpretation of human emotions cannot be arrived at until quite late in the child's development. We have every right to be suspicious of the role that individual experience plays in this connection. In the very young child we usually encounter not only misconceptions about affective manifestations but also indifference to them. Baldwin cites the example of a five-and-a-half month infant who cried when he saw an engraving of a man sitting down, his feet chained, his head in his hands, weeping. This is surprising on two counts: that an infant at that age should manifest a feeling of sympathy; and that he should be able to grasp the meaning of the picture at so early an age. I myself have never observed anything of the kind. But this is not my sole objection to the theory of instinct. How do we explain what Darwin correctly observed (19), that sympathy is usually limited to those individuals who are the object of someone's affection, to the members of a community rather than to the species? The community is distinguished from the species by the significance that individual experience has lent to the perception of certain special beings. One must therefore attribute a role to associations or societies that is the result of living together. Sympathy is not as simple a phenomenon as it is generally believed to be. Especially in the child, it is not so subordinate to affective human cues that it cannot address itself to all kinds of familiar beings — animals and inanimate objects. Yet, likewise in the child, sympathy is sufficiently independent of these cues to allow him, in many instances, to show indifference, especially to strangers. It is not enough to maintain that this is due to displaced attention or to the pull of antagonistic affective tendencies, with the strongest masking the weakest. One must concede that a positive condition which can help to arouse sympathy is simply lacking.

We are familiar with the curious problem Fechner raised. Suppose a child has been reared by a person who always looks severe when he treats the child kindly and smiles when he mistreats him. What kind of significance will these facial expressions assume in the child's eyes? It is hard to believe that there will not be an inversion of the ordinary meaningful relationships, but this is probably impossible to verify. Current evidence indicates, however, that very young children become quickly accustomed to the strangest physiognomies; they apparently do not have to overcome any marked instinctive biases.

The Effects of Resemblance. These remarks take us back to the ordinary associational concepts that view sympathy as the result of individual training rather than as an instinctive predisposition. The principle is one of affective transference. The attitude or physiognomy of others acquires an affective significance for the child because it is associated with real emotions. But this principle can be interpreted in two ways.

First, we may presume that this is a matter of association based on the similarity between expressive phenomena. Generally accepted is the notion that we perceive in ourselves both subjective emotions and phenomena relating to objective expression, whereas in others we perceive only the latter. But since these do resemble our own, they cause us to imagine or feel the corresponding state of mind.

Having thus criticized the theories of imitation, I need not dwell on the point. In any case, this thesis may be acceptable if, in our own emotions, the twofold perception — objective and subjective — is real. At the very same time that we feel our joy or suffering, we also hear our laughter or our outcries. But usually the perception of our attitude and physiognomy comprises only insignificant visual elements, whereas perception of the emotion of others remains purely visual. And the difficulties in perceiving a similarity are even more evident here than in the corresponding theory of imitation. Our usual behavior in our own emotions is perhaps the aspect of ourselves about which we know the least. We rarely have occasion to examine it in a mirror. If we happen to do so, we sometimes feel surprised at the way we look. Can we visualize a child studying the play of his facial expressions like an actor, and noticing some sort of analogy between these expressions and the expressions of others that might conceivably give him the key to their emotions?

Let us pass over this difficulty. We still need to know whether the memory of our emotional mimicry, assuming that it can be evoked by the sight of something analogous in others, possesses an affective value in itself, independently of any notion associated with a particularly moving situation. At the very outset of this discussion, we questioned the contention that the effects of movement in our consciousness will determine the reproduction of movement. Can't the same thing be said about the effects of affective reactions? Imitation of emotional attitudes usually remains unemotional, or else it is affected by some emotional factor in the child himself. This is often true of external, acquired signs of affection, of attitudes of compassion. Very often what predominates in the child is a personal feeling of joy. This stems from pride in his own activity, from the importance of the role he plays, and the signs of admiration or gratitude he receives. When L (2 years) spoke consolingly to her mother or brother in response to signs of affliction, whether real or simulated, was she really sympathizing with them in their unhappiness? I very much doubt this. Little by little, however, genuine feeling will make its way into this little comedy as L's own affective experience increasingly permeates her perception of the external signs of sorrow in others.

The Effects of Contiguity. Thus, the process of educating sensitivity is not determined by an association based upon the similarity of apparent signs of emotion. We must therefore conclude that what is involved is an association or transference based on contiguity. The attitude of others, the circumstances that characterize their affective life, become capable of touching the child because they are consonant with his own real emotions.

In a theory that has become classic, Spencer (67) explains sympathy by the association that is established between subjective impressions and perception of the attitudes of others. Such association, he adds, occurs when several similar beings, subject to the same external influence, respond with the same emotions. A flock of birds, frightened by the sudden appearance on an enemy, takes flight. The sound of the beating wings of the first birds will ultimately have an emotional impact and will frighten other birds that had not noticed the danger. The underlying assumption here is that this reaction is not innate.

Let us cite a few examples illustrating the application of this principle. To begin with, under the heading of sympathy we may classify those instances in which the child and other people are subjected to the same influences through the intermediary of certain objects (we eat the same cakes, smell the same flowers, etc.). Impressions are connected with the object; the use made of it by another person initially serves merely as an additional factor. P (14 months) cried when we approached an object about which he felt a certain apprehension; then *he went away*. Of primary importance was the frightening object. The fact that a familiar person approached it only helped to reinforce his own impression. When he saw me washing myself in cold water, to which he was greatly averse, he said "enough!" and *went away*. He also said "enough" when he was being washed against his will (14:25). A little later, when we alluded in his presence to someone whose foot hurt, he pointed to his own foot and said plaintively, *"bobo"* (16:22).

This equivocal character of the first manifestations of an infant's sympathy will recur later. It will be more momentary and more uneven, because the child will learn very quickly to distinguish among the various people who surround him; we repress or correct the impulses in which our perceptions have been expressed (just as one protects oneself from a blow aimed at someone else, or as one places one's hand on that part of one's own body that corresponds to the place where another person has been hurt).

Sympathetic Participation. The transition from this state to one that might be called *sympathetic participation* takes place without our being aware of it. It should be viewed as the assimilation of an incomplete or inhibited imitation — as the state of mind of an observing spectator who does not himself act. We are not referring to the kind of observation in which the subject remains master of himself and is prepared to react to the object of his observations; rather, we mean attentiveness in which this object becomes "a kind of absolute fascinator," to borrow a phrase from Delacroix (20). Momentarily, the subject forgets about himself and is absorbed in the object of his attention. Isn't this kind of observation characteristic of our perception of *people* whose acts and attitudes we might *imitate*? For example, the attentiveness of the listener who "hangs on every word" of an orator or singer. This is what we mean by mental or sympathetic participation. It is as if we ourselves are impelled by the limbs or voice of another. If we were to characterize this condition otherwise than by metaphor we would have to say that a partial inhibition of acts is involved. All the intermediaries between this attitude and actual imitation are present. We know that deliberate control is not exerted with equal ease over all our movements. In partial inhibition, the first movements to disappear are those that are the most conscious, the most deliberate. The remaining reactions are associated ones.

We know less about how to regulate and reproduce these separately; they constitute the motor residuum of sympathetic participation.

No matter how absorbed a spectator might be in the athletic contest he is witnessing, he will never go so far as to imitate completely the gestures of the players. But sometimes one notices in the spectator involuntary, associational muscular contractions as he watches a player recover his balance. For example, people watching discus throwers do not thrust their own arms forward, but many of them irresistibly and unconsciously follow the body movements of the discus thrower as he leans forward, raises his right leg and brings his full weight to bear on his left leg. This unconscious movement on the part of the spectator betrays a psychic participation in the entire spectacle that manages to elude inhibition. More generally, in these spectacles, the physical effort stimulates muscular contractions which are reflected in the spectators' faces, in the rhythm of their breathing, and in the static quality of their movements.

Without prejudging the nature of the reactions that serve as a basis for affective states of mind, we must observe that affective perception operates here like involuntary motor participation. It is even less subject to the influence of inhibition. It persists beyond any observable participation in external movements. The spectators who watch people dance, who crowd around a gambling table, or who avidly gather to watch some dramatic happening on the street *see* the emotional aspects of the acts they are witnessing as if they themselves were executing them. To watch others perform is one way of satisfying one's own need to perform. In the beginning at least, the spectator forgets about himself. This seems to be the state of mind of the child as he watches acts that interest him, when certain mental complications begin to diminish his eagerness to imitate. Sympathetic participation is a residual condition of total imitation.

Thus, circumstances that promote true or mental imitation lend an affective significance to imitation just as they endow example with the suggestive attributes of motor activity. Some detail of expression or attitude exerts a moral influence on the entire scene. Gestures which the observer can imitate assume for him a coloration of sorts, an affective resonance. The older a child becomes, the more light this theory will shed on the history of his psychic education. Participating more fully in social life, he will find more and more opportunities to live in harmony with those around him. I have, however, presented this theory in so simple a form that it will explain only some of the facts that affect adults as well as the child.

II

The Heterogeneity of the Social Group. When the group reacts in a uniform manner to external influences, the attitude of some becomes a cue that calls the attention of others to the external phenomena and also takes on their affective value. Through the intermediary of his fellowmen, the individual's act responds and adapts itself to these external events. The same is not true of the internal reactions of the group itself, viewed as a composite of heterogeneous individuals. For the individual observing it, an expression is primarily an indication of the observed person's attitude toward the observer. The latter adapts himself to it, responds to it. In general, he does not adapt himself or respond to the circumstances that caused this mental attitude in others, either because he knows nothing about these circumstances or because he is indifferent to them.

This heterogeneity of both functions and needs is a common feature of social relations. Before it becomes an ensemble of similar beings who imitate one another, society — the family, for example — is an ensemble of different human beings who complement and help each other without any immediate equality or reciprocity. And this is precisely what constitutes the equivocal nature of those feelings that are classified under the heading of sympathy. They are replete with the most spontaneous and forceful sentiments which other human beings inspire in them — sexual, paternal or maternal, gregarious tendencies. Each of us is for everyone else something quite different from an exact reproduction of himself. This is no longer a matter of affective resonance but of *reactions* in which the individual obeys special instincts. This emotional diversity is evident in affective antagonisms: rivalry, envy, jealousy, fear, rage. But it is scarcely less real in love, pity, and cooperation. It is not by means of "sympathy" that an animal feeds its young and protects them from danger; no real or possible assimilation is involved here.

This theory has only a limited scope, especially when applied to the child. The affective world of the small child consists mainly of the people around him. States of mind and functions are different in this world. Each is an *object* for the others, one that responds to certain special needs and appears to be the agent of some particular service. The mother is the person who smiles, fondles, and protects; the nurse is the living feeding bottle; the first friends are animated toys. It is this that lends to people's gestures and physiognomy an interest and meaning that usually are quite independent of the feelings they may have or of the cause of these feelings.

The Smile. One may presume that the infant and his mother are delighted by the same object and that consequently the attitude of one acquires a significance for the other. But the complicating factor here is that the object that mainly elicits the mother's pleasure and smile is the child, especially when he smiles. Inversely, it is the sight of the mother and particularly the smiling attention she gives him that elicits the child's pleasure and his smile. If the mother's smile is not in itself the immediate cause of the infant's smile, of his pleasure — and this is why I have rejected the theory of instinct — then it is the physical care accompanying it that primarily determines the infant's joy. In this connection the mother is both the human being expressing emotion at the child's presence and the external cause of his own emotion. It is the maternal instinct itself that insures the normal connection between these two facts.

A closer analysis of the smile is now in order. I observed, although very fleetingly, L's smile on the second and fifth days, after she had been nursed. During the next few days a smile again appeared while she was sleeping or when she was diverted, but never when we talked to her or when she looked at us attentively. On the ninth day, she smiled at me for the first time when she saw or heard me, but always after she had been nursed. On the sixteenth day we noticed a smile after she had been nursed and had fallen asleep — in other words, during the probable absence of any differentiated perception. One week later we managed to make her smile *before* she was nursed, after her underclothes had been removed and we were caressing her legs or brushing her hair with a very soft brush; and also when we came very close to her and spoke to her (22d and 25th days). On the twenty-seventh day she smiled when her mother, brother, or I spoke to her, but she did not smile when spoken to by strangers. This test became easier at 1:12 when she saw the same familiar faces, when there was talking or laughing around her. At 1:28 the smile became more frequent. It was addressed not only to people but also to their mirror images and to familiar objects. At 2:6 L even smiled at strangers in the park; at the sight of herself in the mirror; at another child (2:16); at the grimaces her brother made, or at the sight of him dancing (2:24). When we said to her, "Give us a little smile," she complied. At 5:12 she smiled at the sight of a bust, of an infant's picture which we pretended to caress, of her doll, which we kissed, etc. At 9:5 we often noticed that we could make her smile merely *by smiling* in her presence.

In this evolution, which I have deliberately described in detail, we find first of all physiological excitations (satiety) or physical caresses. But the perception of the people around the baby is associated with efficient circumstances: their physiognomy, their words become in themselves causes for pleasure. Soon the infant smiles not only because of the tonic effect of having been fed, but even when he is not being spoken to or caressed. The mere sight of other people smiling brings on his smile. And why should it be otherwise? All those who try to make a baby smile, using certain effective ways of doing so (words, cajolery, games), *are themselves smiling*. This factor, which is always constant, is first a supplementary, then a sufficient cause. Henceforth it acquires affective significance.

At this juncture we might venture the same observations we made concerning the way the eyes follow an indicated direction. If we assume that the child and the people around him react to an identical situation by expressing an identical emotion, then the child's visual perception will very quickly in itself be sufficient to suggest this emotion. But, generally speaking, this learning process is acquired earlier and more indirectly, at least in a child surrounded by manifestations of interest and affection. The affective state of mind in such a child is expressed by his smile whenever people smile at him. Far from being artificial, this learning process is firmly grounded both in parental instinct and in the child's dependence on the adult as his principal source of satisfaction.

Fear. Fear plays a major role in emotions that are contagious. It is extremely difficult to define precisely the instinctive forms of fear. We have already detailed the infant's first reactions to it. They are apparently caused by sudden sounds, even slight ones, whether he is awake or asleep; coughs, the noise of a key turning in a lock, a door banging, the clapping of hands, a small detonation, a hand rubbing against the wall (from the 4th or 5th day to 3:27); the sudden lighting of a lamp (L, 16 days), an object suddenly thrust toward the infant's face (P, 3:17), or an abrupt transition from light to darkness (very slight reaction). Further causes of fear are strange or unusual perceptions, and changes in familiar objects. The infant's reactions range from a slightly cautious attitude to thrusting himself backward or pushing away with a hand, gestures possibly accompanied by cries, tears, the corners of the mouth turning down, etc. Such reactions occur at the sight of strangers, especially if they come close to the infant wanting to talk to him or pick him up, or when the infant is taken to a strange and dark apartment, etc. (L, 2 months, 2:7, 3:28, etc.). When an infant sees animals, especially stationary ones, curiosity is the dominant emotion. L (6 months) looked serious and guarded when she saw unfamiliar animals (cats, dogs, horses, cows, chickens, butterflies). She refrained from impulsively touching a cat or a horse but was willing to allow us to guide her hand in patting an animal. P (5 months) wanted to pat a dog; he let the dog sniff his face. At six months he himself patted a cat or a horse. He wanted to hold a chicken and was frightened only when the chicken struggled to get away from him.

The seeds of instinct develop as a consequence of experience. An object which thus far has awakened no reaction in an infant may one day seem sufficiently different to arouse his fears. Thereafter he will be afraid each time he sees the object. A familiar animal can suddenly arouse fear because of its sudden movements, especially if these movements are directed *toward* the child. A child beginning to walk approaches a big cat, which runs away. We call the cat. It comes back. The child stops and backs away, a serious expression suddenly appearing on his face.

We can also assume, and this often happens, that certain life situations arise that instill fear in both the adult and the child. Signs of fear in the adult will be significant to the child. But here, too, the facts are more complex. Indeed, certain emotional expressions on the faces of familiar adults directly affect the child and produce in him a distress that seems due, at least in some instances, to primary, instinctive emotional elements which these expressions involve: the suddenness of movements, shouts, or merely unexpected changes in a person's manner or expression.

False Sympathy. Induced sentiments are very often quite different from initial ones. Laughter can provoke anger, shame, or sadness. The sight of someone in pain can provoke irritation, concern, or hilarity. The normal response to anger is fear; the normal response to indifference is sadness or anger. In early infancy some of these phenomena may deceive an observer. He may entertain the illusion that he is witnessing genuine sympathy.

Very young children become agitated and scream or cry when they see their parents upset or in pain, or when they witness feigned ill-treatment of members of their family. By these reactions they are expressing *fear* much more than sadness and pity. An unusual spectacle, especially one involving the child's intimates, tends to produce concern in him. The feelings of the child are somewhat akin to those of an adult witnessing the convulsions of a sick person or the gestures of a madman, or hearing the death rattle, especially if he is quite unaccustomed to such things. Of all the feelings that the highly diverse emotions of those closest to the child might arouse, fear is the most usual. The shouts of other children, an unusual voice inflection when people are conversing, the anger of adults as well as their suffering, even their joy if it is expressed loudly — all these engender anxiety in a child.

For example, I talk to P (4:7) who listens, laughing. Then I happen to burst out laughing, poking fun at him. Suddenly the corners of his mouth turn down; he begins to scream, then to sob. It takes a while to quiet him. He looks at me from time to time, anxiously. Finally, after I speak gently to him, he smiles and his worried expression disappears. A little later the same thing happens when he hears his mother and the maid laughing. At first what he hears are sounds similar to anger; the burst of laughter has a more familiar ring, less distressing to him but nonetheless unpleasant. On the other hand, L (7 months), roundly scolded by her mother, whose breast she has bitten, is also given a slight tap on the cheek. At first she is taken aback. After a few seconds, the corners of her mouth turn downward and she bursts into tears, then begins to shriek. These two examples are actually far less different from one another than one might think. We must not attribute to a child the complicated feelings we would experience in his place under similar circumstances. A child's reaction is one of ·fear, disappointment, and anger when faced with an attitude that *he does not understand* and therefore finds distressing.

When physical ailments or a keen anxiety momentarily lend a strange or unusual quality to a familiar person's manner, tone of voice, or looks, thereby arousing fear in the child, the latter is merely feeling a false kind of sympathy. The same is true when the adult's situation provokes anger in the child because it deprives him of the attention he is accustomed to receiving. If, however, the child shows sadness when he is deprived of caresses and joy when he is caressed once again, something like the quality of sympathy may be ascribed to his feelings. In this case, there is indeed something analogous to sympathy in the affective tonality, even though the feeling is related to different causes, and even though the child is unaware of both the causes and the state of mind of other people. The intellectual content and inherent tendencies of the emotion are altogether different. Complete sympathy does not exist until the similarity comprehends the entire affective state.

Thus, the child may react to the real or feigned emotions of another person. But any affective parallelism between the two is purely accidental. The child's feelings are determined by his special relationship to the other person as well as by the way a given situation reacts upon this relationship or affects the child's habits and well-being.

Egocentric Sympathy. We may call this kind of pseudosympathy egocentric sympathy. This, however, does not mean that it is necessarily selfish, in the usual sense of the word, although it may, to be sure, often take that form. Nevertheless, in an "affectionate" child egocentric sympathy will soon grow broader. In addition to his need for physical care and material well-being, the child will feel that he must have caresses, smiles, words, attention, the mere presence of the other. All these signs of the other person's interest, which, in the beginning, answer a superficial need, will ultimately become far more important to the child than the early gratifications which they foreshadowed.

At first the indications of the inner life of other people interest us only insofar as such evidence seems to affect us. The affectionate child does not put himself *in another person's place*. Holding firm to his own place, he nonetheless thinks more about other people. Certain kinds of relations between him and others have become indispensable and are a source of great satisfaction to him. Anything that troubles or disturbs these relations causes the child uneasiness and suffering. If certain natural, keen affective needs are a primordial precondition of sympathy, then it is in this sense that one can allude to the instinctive root of sympathy. The child's behavior and his feelings toward food and protection seem, in effect, to be dominated by his own instincts. It is altogether possible that one must also take into account the gregarious instinct as well as early forms of parental instinct (attitude toward babies, playing with dolls); perhaps even the sexual instinct in disguised form — if we are to believe the Freudians — comes into play in this connection.

It is extremely difficult to make these concepts more exact or to define the perceptions with which primitive affective reactions are linked. These instinctive reactions do not represent true sympathy; only quite fortuitously do they lead to any kind of affective parallelism. Moreover, even when a certain unity of emotional tonality is achieved, the child's impressions remain inadequate in terms of intellectual content. Experience will enable him to become more unerring in regard to both emotional and intellectual tonality and to develop little by little a genuine form of sympathy. Finally, there is nothing in his instinctive behavior to indicate clearly that other people are anything more for the child than extremely interesting *objects*, or that he has transcended the level of affective *experience*. When P watched his nurse pretend to beat a young girl, he seemed to approve of this. When the roles were reversed, he cried (12:20). In this example, the nurse appears to be an integral part of the sphere of the *mine* rather than another *me*. In another instance, P, crying, sought comfort in the nurse's arms. This is indeed a curious kind of sympathy: the person who is in no way threatened asks the victim to protect him!

III

Sympathy as Knowledge. At what point does the interest the child feels in the attitudes of his familiars become transformed into an *awareness of their inner life*? First, I must explain what I mean by this expression, which seems equivocal. As part of the vocabulary which psychologists employ, it refers to objective and subjective matters. The child can penetrate fairly deeply into the objective behavior of others — the play of their facial expressions and attitudes. Not only are all these things familiar to him, but he also knows something about their logical sequences: a smile, a frown, a scolding or gentle tone of voice that may foreshadow either caresses or rebuffs. This adds up to half of our psychological knowledge about others — perhaps the more important half. But such knowledge does not enable the child to distinguish other persons from objects, save to the extent that people arouse his interest. It does not imply a projection of subjective elements derived from personal awareness (the *Einfühlung* to which the Germans allude), which serves to round out and complete genuine sympathy.

It is a commonplace to say that the child projects his own inner life onto all beings; that with all the animism of primitive man, he sees will, sensitivity, and knowledge everywhere. This is a questionable way of expressing an indubitable fact. In order to remove any equivocation, we must isolate two phases. The first involves no genuine externalization, no tendency to attribute awareness to people or to inanimate objects. It is merely the result of the spontaneous convergence of all the elements of an "experience" that has not yet been analyzed. This phase occurs before the time when subject and object are distinguishable from one another. It takes place at the mental level of experience, not at the level of conceptual thought. I can only define it in negative terms. The second phase is a genuine function which, even as it becomes more precise, finally tends, after some vacillation, to limit itself to man, or to entirely individualized objects that resemble the subject as he knows himself to be — objects that can play the same role he himself plays, or else enter into relationships exactly like his own. What we have here is a genuine assimilation that was lacking before.

The confusion that prevails here arises because the initial phase has not been studied in its primitive form, in the very young infant. Rather, it has been explored in the child who is already able to speak or even beyond that stage. Such explorations were undertaken in connection with attempts to analyze esthetic sympathy wherever a trace of it is to be found.

But what was being studied then in the name of *projection, sympathy, Stimmungseinfühlung* was much more the refraction of this state in the conceptual sphere, in the domain of language — something actually unsuitable for its expression. This can only produce contradictions incompatible with clarity of thought, wherein subject and object are definitely distinguishable. In this context language took the form of grammatical paradoxes, deliberate personifications, and symbols that, because of their very precision, transcend the impression one attempts to describe. It was also expressed in somewhat meaningless discussions about the problem of determining whether feelings are attributed to things or to ourselves. Any analytical method worthy of the name is hardly likely to add to the existing confusion. A frightened child does not project his fear onto the spectacle any more than he locks it within himself. While in the throes of experiencing fear, the child does not distinguish between a frightening object and a frightened subject. This is a life situation in which feeling has not yet become the object of thought.

The Role of Imitation. Consequently, to attribute an inner life to others is not, as has been thought, to extend to other human

beings something one already *knows* about oneself. The inner
life becomes an object of thought only if it is somehow visualized at the very same time that it is being experienced. To put
it differently, only if a child identifies with others who are involved in the same objective situation as he himself is, and only
if they play the same role he plays, can the inner life become an
object of thought. Assimilation is not an extension of the
notion of self, which is assumed to be already formed; rather,
the notion of self is the product of assimilation. The domain
of assimilation becomes more precise as the notion of self becomes defined. These two processes are correlative. Notions
about the subject become more exact with the process being
aided by the image of a certain physical form and by expressive
phenomena. Take two children playing together: their feelings
as well as their actions are dissimilar. They are replicas but not
echoes of one another. The game can be played by reversing
the roles: the agent becomes the patient, the patient the agent.
Each perceives himself in the person of his partner, in the role
he has just relinquished. The active attitude is contemplated;
the feeling experienced is imagined. In this way notions of two
roles are formed (to act and to suffer, to frighten and to be
afraid, to console and to be consoled). At the same time assimilation is limited to those capable of executing complex activities.
The same is true in experiencing physical and psychic interdependence (to receive the same treatment, to share the same
effort). To be sure, once it has sprouted, the idea of self is
naively projected onto others, with all its feelings and motiva-
tions but without the invocation of any rigorous justificatory
analogies. The child does not demonstrate his identity with
other men. We must explain once again what it is that causes
him little by little to emerge from his unconscious egocentricity.
In the preceding example, the child is not involved in relations
based on the dissimilarity of roles (which does not prepare the
way for assimilation); rather, he is involved, at the same time
as another person who is with him, in a relationship with a
third person or with external objects or causes (either as agent

or patient). This kind of situation lends itself to imitation and to assimilation with people.

The final phase of attributing feelings to other people is not actually reached until further intellectual growth occurs. It consists far more in understanding the feelings of others than in sharing them. Moreover, although feeling is in some sense experienced, there is, on the other hand, a negation of its actual and personal qualities. This observation can be understood only by relating it to the mental progress that occurs at that stage of the child's development. He begins to think about matters other than those pertaining to the given, present reality. In thinking about the past, the child imagines and senses the future, the possible. Here there is something of an analogy between the idea of a feeling that one has or might have oneself and the idea of a feeling actually experienced by someone else. In the first instance, one tends to externalize oneself as an object, to visualize oneself in the past or in the future as behaving as one sees other people behave in the present. Isn't the contrast between present experienced tendencies and remembered tendencies one indication of a genuine affective memory, as Ribot claims? In both instances, whether it be sympathy or personal memory, the condition remains unstable, vacillating between two extremes: an exclusively intellectual assessment of the act of ascribing something to someone; an emotion that has once again become actual and personal.

Affective Language. One must also look for indications of affective assimilation in language that is closely linked to certain complex situations. Let us cite a few new examples to supplement the facts already enumerated when we examined the way the notion of self develops.

At twenty-one months P's affective vocabulary included the following words: *happy, naughty, anger, sick, to cry, bobo, to hurt, to want, fear.* All the words were used to allude either to himself or to other people; the lone exception was the word

fear. At the same age, however, his sister used the word *fear* in
both ways.

One of P's first expressions of genuine sympathy (14 months)
was prompted by a baby who was crying. He asked his mother
to nurse the infant: *"Mama! Nénin!"* When he was told, "Nurse
her yourself!" he pinched his clothing around his chest and
seemed about to offer himself to the baby. Upon seeing a woman
nurse her baby, he asked the baby: *"Nénin? Encore?"* (Meaning,
Are you still hungry? 15:26). Upon seeing another baby cry, he
said: *"Nini pleure, bobo, nénin"* (meaning: the little one is
crying, something hurts him, you should nurse him), and he
tried to unbutton his mother's blouse (17 months). Having
bitten a little girl, he explained what he did, albeit in somewhat confused fashion: *"A mord. A pleure. Bobo. Annette"* ("I
bit her, she cried, it hurts her, Annette!"). The language used
makes it plain that complete assimilation was achieved in this
instance. The reference was to situations that are entirely intelligible to the child.

Finnbogason's Theory. Although the role played by imitation
in sympathetic contagion has often been observed, it has not
always been uniformly interpreted. In order to clarify my point
of view, I shall compare it with that of a contemporary psychologist whose theory of imitation has already been examined in
these pages. Finnbogason (25) differentiates between the objective comprehension of other people's attitudes and the tendency to ascribe to them some kind of inner life. Yet he does
admit that the mental content is immediately and directly plain
in the following statement: "I hear the fear of a person who
screams with fear and I see the joy in his smile." Whence does
this mental content spring? From imitation. We understand
others by becoming like them; and we become like them by
imitating them.

Finnbogason fully realizes the difficulty of explaining how
external imitation is transposed and becomes internal imitation, or sympathy. He seeks the basic causes of this transition in

the principle of accommodation. The stimulation of motor mechanisms presumably operates in such a way as to single out the orientation of associations. Not only does the content of consciousness determine our attitudes, but they (which are achieved in some way or other) in turn *appeal* to a certain element in consciousness; and consciousness expresses itself precisely in these selfsame attitudes. Thus, the execution of a rhythmic movement furthers the perception of this particular rhythm, which is one of several. Moreover, the interdependence of all the components of an individual's psychic state is such that a partial accommodation tends to produce a general accommodation. In this way, imitation can be not only intuitive perception but also something creative. Once I have been accommodated, I think, I act, I feel in harmony with the personality of the model such as it appears to be in the manifestation that accommodated me.

Some shrewd observations about mimicry support this exposition, which does, I must concede, have a certain validity. Nevertheless, it strikes me as being a generalization whose scope goes far beyond the hard evidence that can be adduced to substantiate it. If it is accurate, we will have to admit that the phenomenon of sympathy is far less complex that we had thought it to be. To begin with, what is the significance of this insight into a person's soul? The art of mimicry in itself is rather exceptional; therefore it is not likely to yield such a precious intuitive perception. To be sure, we do *believe* that we can detect or hear other people's emotions in their smiles or tears. But of exactly what does this unverifiable impression consist? The person who imitates feels as if he has been pervaded by the personality of the individual he is imitating. But the intensity of this feeling does not prove its authenticity. The idea of the unity of all the elements of a mental state is obviously an exaggeration. Imitation of a physiognomy will change the mimic's voice; he will sense the impossibility of preserving his own voice, or at least so the argument goes. But can he succeed in guessing the real voice? Or, inversely, is he able to go so far as to reconstitute the physiognomy from the voice? How often do the mysterious affinities between the elements of such complex phenomena which we think we feel spring from the persistence in our memory of the very loose bonds of accidental contiguity!

Not all imitation, to be sure, is purely physical. Certain attitudes are permeated with an indefinable psychic quality. But this is something that stems from within us. What we think we perceive in the soul of another is not a revelation of his unique personality; rather, it is something that we ascribe to him but which in reality is a part of ourselves. Among the many and varied states of mind we have personally experienced, imitation can guide us toward the one that most closely resembles the momentary state of mind of the person imitated. Such a method is valid only to the extent that real similarities between the imitator and the model do exist. If such similarities are not present, the method is likely to prove illusory.

Even if this kind of insight into a person whose nature is very alien tc our own should have a certain amount of validity, it will still be necessary to recognize the role played by a specific factor other than imitation: the interdependence (which has become familiar to us through the observation of others) of various objective manifestations of emotion and behavior. The cohesiveness of a certain ensemble of memories — and this is difficult to explain — ultimately acquaints the spendthrift with avarice, the man with the child or the animal, the modest man with the ambitious one. This latent experience plays an important part in the feeling we have that we can perceive a certain logic in the behavior of people, as well as in our own tendency to identify ourselves with whatever is unique or individual in other people.

But let us return to the psychology of the child. One must not exaggerate what the child is able to perceive about the personality of other people by imitating them. His experience is short and summary. Even when he succeeds in copying external things reasonably well, his imitation cannot engender a psychological precociousness. And this is what points up the limitations of the theory of accommodation, which is so very seductive because of its consequences.

Conclusion. Let us resume our discussion. We have discarded the idea that the perception of expressive phenomena can awaken by a direct resonance in the child the feelings that correspond to these phenomena. Nor does such a resonance spring from a direct perception of the analogy with emotional manifestations, of which the subject is generally unaware. On the contrary, there is a good deal of truth in the theory that ascribes to experiential associations not only the affective significance acquired by expressive phenomena as a consequence of perception but also the modifications and refinements of the initial significance of these phenomena. Nevertheless, we cannot confine ourselves to the simple case of similar individuals reacting to the same external factors in an identical fashion. Emotional attitudes usually have a special meaning for the child. The reason for this is his relationship to the person involved, not his relationship to the initial cause of the emotion. The affective parallelism is accidental and produces nothing more than egocentric sympathy. Influenced by everything that furthers assimilation with people, especially imitation, the child evolves beyond this stage. Assimilation progresses from the object to the individual and is ultimately expressed by an intellectual act in which the use of affective language constitutes both the tool and the cue.

IV

Selfish Inclinations in Imitation. In studying imitation, we have mainly examined its intellectual aspects. How *can* the child emulate and verify the correctness of his copy? This question cannot be considered entirely apart from the role of affective circumstances. Example is not merely a model and guide; it likewise serves as a stimulus, operating through the medium of a certain state of mind which I will describe briefly.

I have already dealt critically with the idea of an impulse that will *automatically* and surely activate in a general way the process of imitation. Certain facts make this somewhat plausible. Acts are apparently performed when the mind is in some manner diverted. Preyer, who put his son through a series of exercises in imitating words and syllables, noticed that he was more successful when the child was tired. An instance of this was the way the child performed immediately after struggling against being washed and having to give in. Sometimes a word which the child had not yet imitated was finally uttered absent-mindedly, in a low voice, as if in a dream. Very absorbed by the spectacle of a group of young girls who were doing setting-up exercises, L did exactly as they did when she saw them all raising their legs. Realizing then what she was doing, she laughed. Often, after watching the model but not moving herself, she would suddenly imitate the act, as if her memory had been waiting to be jogged. But one must not exaggerate the role of automatism in the child's behavior. He is, after all, a creature in the throes of development and for him constructive activity and initiative are paramount. Furthermore, this automatism does not in itself exclude the possibility of special inclinations that may also be at play.

One must first take into account the real interest the child has in the act to be imitated. A child watching others play is attracted to whatever game is under way. Concrete example represents the most striking and powerful guise in which the temptation to perform an act occurs to him. It is unquestionably more effective than a spontaneous mental image or a verbal suggestion. But the observer must also take into account both the nature of the example and the personality of the individual setting the example.

An example that tallies with the child's latent inclinations has its own power of seduction, its own prestige. A child does not imitate anything and everything; he does not give himself over with equal enthusiasm or tenacity to any game that might be suggested. Although little boys do play with dolls, they do so with far less eagerness than little girls. Each sex, like each age, prefers to imitate certain models.

It has been demonstrated (Groos [26], Ferretti [24]) not only that imitative games are governed by instincts but also that they owe some of their interest to the special exercise of intellectual activity which they occasion. We have merely to reexamine the numerous examples already cited in the preceding chapters to see that most of these appear to the child in the guise of new *problems* that arouse his curiosity. They also appeal to the child's desire to overcome difficulties, to enlarge his field of knowledge and action, to operate as both the creator and the achiever of definite objectives. And so each imitation reaches its zenith and declines. There comes a time when interest in an act is exhausted, when the inclinations that made it attractive are no longer present and the child is ready to seek fresh stimuli.

But the psychology of imitation is even more complex. Social sentiments must be taken into account. Many examples are imitated only in the presence of an audience. Awareness of the spectator, the wish to attract attention, to arouse admiration, soon come to serve as additional stimuli whose role will grow. As Piaget has shown (50), the small child is in a sense an isolated being; his playing does not at first combine with that of his friends in a complex action. But his mental isolation is not total. Although he feels no need for a partner, he does want an audience. Furthermore, many forms of imitation serve to influence other members of the group. Such, for instance, is the role of language and symbolic gestures. The child quickly becomes mindful of this power.

An interesting feature of the process is that the evolution of these inclinations will later restrict imitation. As early as the close of the second year, a more complicated feeling of self and of the effect one produces on others occasionally exerts an inhibiting influence. We have noted in particular a need for perfection and a sense of shame that paralyzed all initiative and prevented the child from engaging in imitation with the com-

plete naiveté that characterized his first efforts. He was afraid
of appearing ridiculous and distrusted himself. He had acquired
a sense of inadequacy and had become aware of his own ignorance about the situation within which every child operates. Or
else he was afraid that his performance would be compared
unfavorably with that of other children.

The model's personality is also very important. It is not true
that a child always imitates his superiors, in the true sense of
the words. But in his eyes his models do enjoy a certain prestige
which is very difficult to pinpoint. Pessimists have exaggerated
the role played by poor example. The child's perspective differs
from ours.

The child looks upon adults or older friends as his superiors.
He wants to attain their level. The result is imitation of acts
that are meaningless or devoid of interest. The activities of the
adult are infinitely important to the child because of their impact and the variety of their effects. This is the source not only
of the child's astonishment but also of his admiration. As a
consequence, the activities of the adult ultimately arouse a
growing interest in the child for the very reason that an adult
is involved. If I look out the window, the child wants to "see"
the object of my curiosity, which must be interesting, indeterminate though it may be. The one-year-old wants to read and
write. Later, he will enjoy repeating words he does not understand and playing often unintelligible adult roles. The self
which later will seek more subtle satisfactions in personal,
original action at first finds these satisfactions in premature
imitations. All of this is only an affective result of the transference of the suggestive significance of objects to people. Nor are
imitations of the child's inferiors — animals, babies, sick people — unrelated to this need for self-assertion. The sense of the
comic, as we know, is clearly connected to one's feeling of
superiority.

Therefore we should not seek the point of departure in a
general imitative instinct, which explains everything and
nothing, even what is unreal. Rather, we should look for it in

the special instincts that the circumstances of social life and the experience they determine direct toward the path of imitation.

Envy and Jealousy. An examination of envy, emulation, or jealousy will lead to the same conclusions. What is involved here is an instinctual root which we may call, for lack of a better term, the instinct of self-assertion, of appropriation. But the feeling becomes clear only when an obstacle appears in the more definite form of a human rival *identified* with the subject.

The indifference of very young infants in those circumstances most likely to stir their feelings is no less striking than the passion they will feel a little later. Thus P (3:20 to 3:23), and his sister at the same age, showed the utmost indifference when I pretended to seize their mother's breast in their presence. The first examples of passionate involvement appeared in P (9:4) and in L (7:19), that is, precisely at the same time as their first imitations; thereafter, and under the most diverse circumstances, they multiplied.

Envy at first is only a crude way of expressing desire for an object; it is capable of arousing desire in other circumstances. Let us suppose that an object was seen in someone's hands when the child had reached a certain age. The tendency to imitate will reinforce the suggestion that stems from the object itself. Even if a child is not hungry, he will be envious of the piece of cake someone else is eating. Doubtless in animals this feeling has an instinctual root that is independent of everything that experienced reality has taught them. Be that as it may, children soon become envious of an object to which they had remained indifferent until someone else obtained possession of it. The object seems desirable only because it is coveted by someone else. P (14:18) was playing with friends. They spent practically all their time grabbing objects from one another.

Envy implies action involving two persons. Genuine jealousy requires the presence of a third person. In the latter instance, the object to which the tendency refers is one that the child's desire and his rival's action have in common; it is no longer a thing but a person. As this notion becomes more precise, the feeling itself attains greater distinctiveness.

Envy and jealousy exist from the moment we see a person in possession of a privilege that is denied us, whether this pertains to a thing or to an individual. Both envy and jealousy are felt most keenly whenever the objects involved are those we consider to be our very own. Thus, for the child, his toys, his clothes, his house, his parents, and above all the acts that usually center on him, can become objects of envy or jealousy. It is precisely because his rival appears to be imitating him, because the assimilation is total, that the rival ceases to be an ordinary obstacle to the satisfactory fulfillment of his desire. The same spectacle that stimulates the greatest activity radically inhibits this very same activity. Both mental participation and a distressing sense of being stymied are present. The intellectual state of mind comes close to a feeling of sympathy; we know that transitional phases exist. The affective state changes because inhibition is intolerable.

The first indications of jealousy in my children were noted when they were being nursed or caressed. At first a simple desire was aroused by the mere sight of the act. P (3:25), in the presence of his mother, expressed a desire to be nursed when he saw a baby being nursed; L (3:18), in the same circumstances, wanted to go up to a complete stranger who was nursing her baby and seize the woman's breast (but without giving any sign of wishing to suck it). It is difficult to say whether it was the sight of the breast or the act of nursing that produced such a reaction. This tendency, which typically occurs when latent desire is aroused, remains characteristic for a long time. It is only later that jealousy will become a simple emotional state suffused with inactive mental suffering, or that it will express itself by directly hostile attitudes. Nor is there any characteristic jealousy when, at that same stage or a little later, the baby becomes irritated because no attention is paid to him, or because other people or other things deprive him of attention. On the other hand, P (9:28) was jealous when his mother pretended to kiss me, or when she put her head on my shoulder (10:13). He tried to thrust himself between us.

There comes a time when children are able to accept the idea of sharing demonstrations of affection or the activities of a rival. Occasionally, the child is willing to accept caresses from some other person. When L's mother caresses her brother, she comes into my arms. Generally speaking, jealousy disappears as a consequence of personal action that serves as a distraction. The child is willing to offer the cake he did not want to his rival.

But the distinctive characteristic of envy and jealousy is a certain attitude either toward the envied *person* or toward the individual of whom one is jealous and not only an attitude toward the *object* of the desire.

At first this person is only an obstacle to the execution of an act. When the child tries to slip between his mother and myself, I am a material obstacle to his act. This may result in ordinary reactions of disappointment or anger. The distinctive characteristic of envy and jealousy stems from the fact that the obstacle is *assimilated* to the self: it usurps our place and plays our role. But there are degrees of assimilation. P (9:21) snatches his doll from our hands and throws it away when we caress it. Does he do so because it is an ordinary object that draws our attention away from him? Or does he see in the doll a rival usurping the caresses due him? At a somewhat later stage the second interpretation would probably be the correct one, but at this date it is not easy to choose between the two. We know that children are mainly jealous of other children of the same age, as well as of anyone with whom they can identify themselves closely. L and P were very jealous of their dolls. P threw his away whenever we pretended to caress it. L (21 months) did not want anyone to make dresses for her doll. She would scream with rage: "She has dresses!" Children affected by poor health or a need for attention or activity, sometimes surprise us by the way manifestations of jealousy follow close on the heels of sympathy. While her brother P lay on his mother's lap, L rocked the chair on which the parent was sitting (12:30). A few days later the same spectacle produced a sudden fit of jealousy.

Finally, in my previous allusion to genuine jealousy I called attention to the appearance of a third person and all the complications that this entails. After a certain age such attitudes are interpreted by the child himself. He begins to be preoccupied with the feelings of the loved one toward himself and toward the person of whom he is jealous. L, who was extremely jealous of her brother during the initial months of the third year, often asked: "Do you love me, Mama? You don't love P?" At this stage, also, she often went into a corner, brooding and feeling humiliated instead of trying to take her rival's place. But, and this is typical of her age, she did not extend to the loved one the hostile feelings she entertained toward the person who was the cause of her jealousy.

IMITATION IN ANIMALS

I

The Problem. Although what I have been saying so far does not pertain to animal behavior, I must now attempt to ascertain whether my description of the child is confirmed by current data on animal psychology. If we discard anecdotes that are either questionable or difficult to interpret, we have little left in the way of knowledge about the problem of imitation in animals. Only by combining experimentation with observation is it possible to arrive at an accurate evaluation of the conditions that must obtain if example is to influence the behavior of animals. We must eliminate instances of pseudoimitation where a common stimulus determines similar acts that occur independently of one another among several individuals. We must make a distinction between instinctual and acquired imitation and also clarify the mechanism involved in the latter process. The numerous researches on this subject have not always yielded results that can be reconciled with each other.

Let us first eliminate the vague question of mimicry which has occasionally been associated with imitation. Under the heading of imitation, two sets of facts have been grouped.

1. Morphological data: permanent similarities of form, pattern, and coloration among animals belonging to different species; such similarities between an animal and an object (leaf, branch) or between elements of the milieu where the animal lives.

2. Physiological data, or the momentary changes by means of which the animal achieves a varied adaptation: The best known example is that of the pleuronectids, who adapt them-

selves to whatever milieu in which they are placed. We know that the effect achieved is due to contractions of their pigmented spots, which make the tegmenta look at times lighter, at others darker. These contractions are produced by a reflex whose point of departure is a visual stimulus. This brings us much closer to authentic imitation.

The concept of imitation becomes more precise when the act or attitude of a living being is patterned after that of a similar living being. Perception of the latter determines the execution of the act of the former. We will employ the method already used in studying the child. First we will examine vocal imitation and then move on to the general problem.

Vocal Imitation. MacDougall concedes that vocal imitation should be given a very special place because it is the most authentic, perhaps the unique, example of imitation in animals. Here indeed one essential precondition invariably exists: homogeneity of the perceptions of the model's acts and of the acts of the subject that imitates the model. The bird can compare its song with that of other birds. The problem, however, is far from simple, involving as it does an extremely complicated mixture of instinctive and acquired data.

The following observations plainly demonstrate that a certain number of vocal manifestations characteristic of a determinate species appear in individual animals, independently of the influence of example and presumably because of organic or affective conditions.

Boutan (7) raised a gibbon (*Hylobates*) which he had taken from its natural habitat at an early age. He kept it five years. At no time did it see any other member of its own species. Five months after its arrival in France, it developed an affective language identical with that of its species. This language consisted of three categories of sounds expressing well-being or satisfaction, uneasiness or fear, and finally, a state of excitation.

The Norwegian naturalist Schjelderup-Ebbe (59), who devoted ten years to a study of the domesticated hen, distinguished thirteen kinds of sounds that were either common to the species or specifically associated with one of the sexes. Each cry not only had its own determinate form (rhythm, pitch, intensity), but was also associated with certain instinctual acts or situations (various stages of the hatching process, fighting, coupling, alarm, calls, etc.). Each cry appeared at a given moment in the hen's development and at a precise date, regardless of whether it happened to be isolated from the species or in the presence of individual adults (with one exception to which I shall in due course return).

Craig (17) made similar observations about pigeons raised in isolation. Among songbirds a distinction must be made between genuine song and cries or chirps (calls for help or sounds of alarm). Generally speaking, preformation is much more pronounced in the bird's chirps than in its song. The chirps never require any prior training and usually persist without any change. Mitchell, however, has noted that they can be modified to a certain extent. Scott (60), who raised as many as sixteen different species of birds in one room, observed that the cry for help sometimes persists and sometimes becomes unrecognizable.

Conradi (15), who raised a young sparrow with canaries, pointed out that the sparrow's first chirp for food, after a normal start, gradually lost its crude quality until it came to resemble the peep of the young canaries.

But the bird's song more than anything else is subject to influence. Scott (60) isolated some Baltimore orioles before they had heard the song of the species. He kept them under observation for several years. They finally developed into good singers, but their song was not at all like that of their species, save for their cackling. Among sixteen kinds of birds thus isolated from adult members of their own particular species, but exposed to the songs of the other birds inside and of birds outside, not once was a typical or normal song ever heard.

Conradi noted that all the sparrows raised with canaries had learned to sing by imitating the latter. The sparrows whose song was pitched at a higher, more musical level, had learned to warble. In a few instances, "except for musical polish," the imitation was perfect. But once they were separated from the canaries and heard the sparrows outside, two of these birds lost their ability to sing and resumed the sparrow chirp (within two and a half months), although they retained a more musical quality. Within a few weeks after they had been returned to the room with the canaries, they recovered all they had lost.

The example of the parrot shows that this kind of imitation can go much further. The parrot that Lashley (38) observed began to speak when it was nine months old. First it imitated a trained parrot, then a man. Lashley made a detailed inventory of everything the parrot was able to reproduce: guttural sounds, coughing, and whistling were well imitated; smacking the lips was also reproduced but not quite as perfectly. Musical sounds (violin, cello, piano, the human voice whistling or singing) were imitated with whistling or singing sounds but without any reproduction of the tone of these instruments. The imitation of the pitch was obvious although somewhat capricious. But the parrot could not repeat a short melody it heard for the first time.

We need not dwell on the fact that the production of sound is closely dependent on the nature of the vocal apparatus. What interests us far more is the subordination of possible sounds to certain causes. We have called attention to the essential role played by organic and affective causes. Imitation is possible only to the extent that auditory perception is either a principal or an auxiliary stimulus. It is remarkable that the vocal sounds made by animals should loom so large in their social relations. Quite apart from the domain of instinct, such sounds become, in certain instances at least, a secondary stimulus. The sound made by one animal is a response to the sound made by a similar animal, stereotyped in form but at that precise moment excited by auditory perception. The rooster spontaneously emits his characteristic crow (cock-a-doodle-doo!) under the influence of some kind of affective impetus about which we know nothing. But the sound made by another rooster reinforces or provokes anew this same impetus, and the first rooster answers the second. This probably explains why — in contrast to the manner in which other cries are produced — the sounds made by older animals hasten by twenty or thirty days the first emission of the young rooster's characteristic crow. We can see of course why the role of auditory perception tends to become preponderant among other species. There exists a semblance of imitation as a consequence of the fact that the cries of all kinds of animals are stimulated by the cries of animals of the same species. This becomes even more striking if the species is noted for certain variations in the sounds its members use to call one another; in every instance they are answered in like fashion.

Nevertheless, in order to explain authentic imitation, which molds primitive reactions to a variety of types presented by the model and which eventually may transform the specific type into forms of song or articulation alien to it, one must unquestionably assume that something more is involved: a function analogous to that which I have described in the child and which I have called self-imitation. This is a tendency to attempt, by means of trial and error, to imitate an auditory model that made its appearance either as a consequence of an accidental personal performance or through the presentation of an alien example. The fact is that all songbirds and all talking birds practice for a long time. They achieve the desired result only through efforts that at first seem quite clumsy but which gradually improve. Conradi noted that the sparrows that learned to sing like canaries apparently showed visible throat movements, although no sound emerged, when they listened to the singing of the canaries. In the parrot, the auditory recording is followed by persistent effort to imitate, often after lengthy intervals. It seems as if here, too, success goes hand in hand with what has been acquired previously.

Besides, this kind of imitation, like all games of which it is only one form, must be backed up by instinctual tendencies. Lashley observed in his parrot a state of excitation and even of hostile fury during the experiments. He discerned a connection between imitation and sexual rivalry (38).

The Gregarious Instinct. Let us turn now to the far more confusing problem of the general imitation of acts and seek to ascertain whether this kind of imitation might be instinctive. All the facts that we shall examine give no support whatsoever to the notion of a general imitative instinct. The first semblance of imitation appears in certain specific instincts, especially in what is called the gregarious instinct. It impels animals of the same species to herd together and to follow one another as they move from place to place.

Doubtless we are listing under the same heading things that are rather different. In order to achieve a better understanding of the gregarious instinct, we must know exactly how the presence of one animal affects the other, what kinds of stimuli are involved, in what way the influence of each is exerted, and which elemental reactions are called into play. We must obviously ascribe a role to smell, sight, and touch. We must also take into account physiological states, influences that are sexual or nutritive in origin, etc. The gregarious instinct is permanent in certain species. In others it is temporary (migrations, the temporary gatherings of mammals, birds, fish) and the consequence of external causes which are not as yet very well understood. Sometimes the gregarious instinct encompasses only the family. The animals remain together when they are young, then they separate. Other groups are composed of individual animals of varying origins, united because of circumstances.

Consequently we must regard the gregarious instinct as a reality whose mechanism is not thoroughly understood. One thing, however, is certain: the initial manifestation of the phenomenon of imitation stems from the gregarious instinct. Animals move together; they follow one another and are therefore exposed to the same influences and subjected to the action of the same situations and the same objects. They react to all

this according to the way they are structured, which further confirms the impression they give of imitating one another.

A multitude of data indicates, moreover, that the actual
stimulus arising from instinct — whatever its specific character
might be — has not the precision one is at first inclined to ascribe
to it. The being from which it emanates acts on the senses of
other animals in a very complex way. Their perception of this
being's form and movements is replete with elements, of which
only a few — and unfortunately these are difficult to discern —
provoke the instinctual response. Everything occurs as if the
image of the model or the specific act — if we can speak meta-
phorically — remains half-obliterated in the ancestral memory.
As we know from our own domesticated animals, a gregarious
animal community is easily established among the young of
various species.

In an animal, the instinct to follow is not dependent on the
perception of a specific form. Cole has noted that young raccoons, as soon as they have learned to walk, exhibit a strong
tendency to follow humans. This tendency begins to diminish
toward the middle of the seventh month and disappears altogether around the middle of the eighth. Hudson has reported
(cited by W. Mitchell) that a horseman riding past young lambs
that had been sleeping was followed by them for several miles
after their sudden awakening by his passage. Doubtless some
defect or anomaly of the instinct accounts for this. But if we
are to record rather than judge such phenomena, we must say
that they constitute an indeterminate instinctual tendency in
relation to the normal object.

Acts Related to Objects: The Development of Habits. The same
conclusion emerges when we examine acts in relation to objects
presented as examples of instinctive imitation. I have already
alluded to the instance of the baby chick which, according to
the observations of some, instinctively imitates the act of pecking when the hen sets the example. The hen itself pecks or picks
up a seed from the ground and lets it fall, emitting at the same

time the clucking sound characteristic of the species. Peal has pointed out that young pheasants would starve themselves to death if no such example were given them. The same thing has been reported about an ostrich raised in an incubator (Morgan [46*a*]). What role should be ascribed to efficiency in the ostrich's perception? First, it should be noted that a chicken raised in an incubator is quite capable of functioning without the benefit of example. Secondly, as Morgan has shown, the act of pecking can be stimulated by striking the ground with the point of a pencil, or by picking up tiny seeds with tweezers and then letting the seeds fall to the ground. The perception of a gesture made by an animal of the same species is therefore not essential. Perception is made up of many elements other than efficiency.

When a baby chick tries to pick seeds up from the ground, its first efforts are quite clumsy. The progress it makes can be traced, as Breed (8) has done, by counting the number of attempts and the number of successes. During the first week of a chick's life, the number of successes increases from 16 percent to 90 percent. The progress curve for chickens raised in an incubator can be compared with the one for chickens who have the example of hens to follow. The results in both cases are virtually identical. The advantage of example is thus shown to be almost nonexistent.

In the young cat, example seems to foster the predatory instinct. The mother brings live mice to her young, releases them, and chases them in front of the kittens. Yerkes studied the attitude toward mice of young cats that had been raised in isolation. They paid no attention to mice during the first four weeks of life. Then one of them chased a mouse, acting out a fully developed type of instinct (chase, capture, growling, toying with the victim, then the kill). By the end of the second month this instinct appeared to be quite independent in all the animals observed.

Craig's observations (16) of pigeons raised in isolation indicate that they do not know how to find water or how to drink. But if the bottom of the water container is pricked with a pencil point, the pigeon will plunge its beak into the water. If the water reaches the inside of its mouth, it will begin to drink. This example illustrates how modest is the role of imitation.

The function of example is therefore plainly an auxiliary one, at any rate insofar as one can draw conclusions from the data I have just analyzed; moreover, the motor valence is connected to only one of its aspects. It may be, however, that because of this other factors acquire a certain importance, at least in higher animals. Perhaps genuine habits are grafted onto instinct, a supposition that would reinforce the notion of imitation. If this is so, then the tendency to herd together or to follow would be related to the perception of a form or of a determinate movement; the gestures of pecking, drinking, etc., would therefore assume a significance quite apart from a given object's appeal. This is somewhat analogous to the transferences I have noted in children. At first, to be sure, the chicken's attitude, when it pecks and lets the grain fall to the ground, serves merely to reinforce whatever influence the stimulus produced by the object may possess. But group living tends to provide a more exact cue; individuals become accustomed to patterning their movements after those of others.

Small (65) and Berry (4) have noted that a rat starts to dig a hole wherever it sees another rat engaged in digging. Kinnaman observed a monkey searching a hole into which it had seen another monkey plunge its arm. Lowering its head, the questing monkey looked first to the right and then to the left. It also jumped onto a table and climbed a tree, each time in imitation of another monkey. Watson (78) has recorded similar observations about monkeys. A mother monkey chased her baby away from a hole so she could look into it herself because she could not see the object from where she had been. Berry (4) caged a white rat with another rat of the same species that knew how to get out of the cage. He found that the first rat followed the second wherever it went. The first rat showed an interest in the mechanism which the second rat manipulated to open the cage. Porter (52) made the same experiment on birds. He noticed that they took a position that enabled them to get out of the cage when the one bird who knew how managed to get the door open. Sometimes they even tried to imitate the maneuver. Nor can we feel any surprise that the chimpanzees Köhler (37) studied showed similar tendencies which made them seem almost human.

It is obvious that such instances of imitation are to be found primarily among social animals. This is so not only because social life fosters transferences but also because the instincts involved in group living constitute an affective basis for such transferences. We have noted the role of the gregarious instinct. Feelings of rivalry or jealousy among beings accustomed to living together do, however, constantly accompany the object's true appeal. This lends a special motor and affective significance to the acts of others.

Does this evolution go even further? Does the object, the result, finally disappear to be replaced by autonomous imitation, as in the child? Liberation of this kind seems to be bound up with the playful activities characteristic of higher animals. This is especially true during their initial years, when instincts as yet incomplete tend to mature and develop fully through practice. Such games often assume the form of self-imitation. A monkey (*Cebus*) observed by Watson (78) amused himself by trying to balance a tablespoon on his extremity. Then he would let the spoon fall. He repeated this game fifteen consecutive times. Watson compared him to the child who bangs on a table with a spoon. Another of the favorite games of this particular monkey was to bang on something with a nut or some other small, hard, preferably round, object. In one instance he repeated the gesture one hundred and fifty times within the space of a single hour. A rhesus monkey played with a small object; he let it fall then picked it up over and over again. Köhler's chimpanzees (36 and 37) played with all kinds of objects, apparently exploring tenaciously any "interesting" result they happened upon in the course of their manipulations. Thus they smeared themselves with colored paints, and wound wires or the straw in their cages together and tied them. They used a variety of objects as ornaments. Under the influence of imitation, some of these games became generalized and were very much in vogue within the small circle of the station.

Constructive Imitation. So far, acts subordinated to the example of others have been limited to the domain of instincts or habits. But can imitation in animals lead to the execution of truly new acts?

In Watson's opinion (77), genuine imitation is "a relatively instantaneous regrouping of old habits." If we accept this definition, it will prove difficult to find examples of genuine imitation in animals. It is not enough that all the elementary movements are familiar; they must also be combined. This, according to Watson, is something that man himself has rarely been able to accomplish. (I cannot imitate a new dance without first practicing it even though all the elementary movements of the dance are familiar to me; but the dance master can.) We can also detect the impact of imitation on attempts of various kinds made through trial and error whereby the accomplishment of an act is achieved under circumstances that will *ultimately* lend it form. The influence of imitation intervenes to *abbreviate* these attempts by narrowing the indeterminate nature of the problem.

In the present state of our researches, it is only fair to say that, in spite of some conflicting results, constructive imitation in animals, at least in the forms we have just defined, is extremely limited in scope.

Imitation of Passive Movements. One method has been to suggest the act by forcing the animal to execute it passively.

Thorndike (72) observed that cats, of their own accord, would enter the door of a cage. Closing this door, he seized one of the cats by the scruff of the neck, held it up, and let it fall through an opening at the top of the cage. He did this to three cats, but not one of them tried on its own to enter the cage from the top (50, 60, and 75 attempts).

Some dogs, some cats, and one monkey (*Cebus*) were tested to see if they would manipulate a mechanism in the cage that opened the door. The experimenter left all these animals alone for a few minutes to see if they would try to get out of the cage. Nothing happened. Then he took their paws and forced them to manipulate the mechanism. He did this several times. The animals were then left to their own devices for ten or fifteen minutes. Thereupon the experiment was repeated. Not once did the animals spontaneously attempt to imitate the passive movement. (We must not forget that by trial and error, these animals finally managed to solve the problem.) It must be pointed out, however, that Thorndike's negative results conflict sharply with the findings recorded in Cole's studies of the raccoon (12). According to Cole, the raccoon passed the first test with flying colors. Finding the door closed, it climbed up the cage and lowered itself into it through the opening at the top.

Nevertheless, it is easy to understand why these experiments usually fail. As Thorndike has noted, the cues provided by an animal's sense must be associated with a motor impulse. If the animal is handled passively by the experimenter, the motor impulse will be lacking. Indeed, any intervention on the part of the experimenter tends to produce inhibitions. I have already indicated that the child, on the contrary, will respond to cues which a passive movement provides. He participates actively. The mechanical suggestion he receives guides the movement but does not cause it.

Imitation of Example. There are other methods that may also be employed. For example, the animal might be given a demonstration of how to execute the act. Or another trained animal could be used to provide such a demonstration. Here too, in spite of a wide divergence of opinion among observers, the method usually proves rather unsuccessful, or else it succeeds only if the most intelligent animals are used for the experiment.

Thorndike was not able to teach a dog how to open a box by operating the mechanism in its presence.

Several cats were removed one after the other from a large cage that opened at the top. They usually climbed close to the opening as soon as the experimenter appeared. But one cat that did not acquire this habit spontaneously failed after eighty attempts to imitate two other trained cats. Two groups of cats were trained to climb up, one group upon the arrival of the experimenter, the other at a given signal. But no single member of one group imitated when it was placed among the others.

Shepherd (62) performed an experiment with a trained raccoon. In order to eat, the raccoon had to reach a platform by walking up a ramp from a box. He could then jump from the top of the cage. But the example set by this raccoon in no way reduced the time it took the other raccoons to solve the problem through trial and error. Yerkes reports that the example of a dancing mouse, trained to get out of a cage through a ladder, did not stimulate the other mice to imitate it. Two groups of mice were trained to open a door, one by pulling, the other by pushing. Neither group ever imitated the act of the other.

By way of contrast to these negative experiments, I should cite a few results considered positive by those who reported them.

Berry (3) holds that the white rat is capable of learning to perform a few imitative acts. He concludes that the presence of one trained white rat that knows how to get out of a cage will accelerate the learning process of other white rats. A cat will not turn a button that will enable it to open the cage door until it has seen another trained cat do so. Berry has likewise witnessed certain acts that were imitated: pushing a ball into a hole, pulling on a knotted cord, etc.

Porter (52) takes the position that imitation may be said to occur when a trained animal changes its manner of performing an act because of the example set by some other animal. He thinks he has observed this phenomenon in the behavior of birds.

Even if such results are regarded as positive, imitation nonetheless appears to be unaccountably limited. It is difficult to make a sharp distinction between imitation and personal apprenticeship. Imitation can find expression in the localization of the field of attention. But the movements of the trained animal, and even more so those of the experimenter, fail completely to stimulate corresponding movements on the part of the animal.[1] The *objects* upon which such action is exerted possess too vague an influence to determine without experimentation the complex and to a certain degree new act that is to be accomplished. In reference to this point, I shall assess the validity of my thesis about an animal's general inability *to copy movements* which it sees executed by another animal of the same species.

Imitation in Monkeys. I have saved for the last an examination of a special group in which imitation has always been thought to play a very important role — monkeys. However, in this group, imitation is not at all what it is usually thought to be.

Thorndike (72) proved unsuccessful in his efforts to teach a cebus monkey how to open a door by one of the two methods described above. On the basis of his findings, he even maintains that the monkey will not return spontaneously to the table to which he is usually carried when he is to be fed.

Watson (78) obtained no results whatsoever in his experiments, although his working conditions seemed propitious. Two rhesus monkeys lived together for several years and seemed to have a great affection for each other. B, the younger, would become wild and agitated when J was away from him. J would emit a special cry when he called B, and would put his arms

1. Thorndike has investigated the role of imitation in the training of animals. But the reports made by four famous animal trainers are not very coherent. They mainly show that there is a great disparity between the practice of an art and the rigorous analysis of its procedures.

around B's neck. B liked to rest against J, winding his arms around J's chest. If B did not quiet down, J would rock and fondle him. Whenever J went to one part of the cage, B would follow. When a bowl of milk was placed on the ground, B waited for J to precede him before drinking. J developed the habit of jumping onto the shoulder of the experimenter when he came in and called him. B acquired the same habit. If, for some reason, J refused to come, B would also refuse. B would not enter the cage unless J preceded him. Nevertheless, Watson was unable to detect any evidence of imitation in the following tests:

1. The two animals were supposed to imitate the experimenter (pulling a piece of fruit with a rake or a sheet; getting a piece of fruit from the bottom of a box with a fork; getting it out with a stick from a glass cylinder open at both ends, etc.).

2. B was supposed to imitate J (J had been trained on the basis of trial and error) in raising a door by a handle, and in opening a door by pulling a knob.

Noteworthy is the fact that despite the failure of example to exert any noticeable influence, the monkeys quickly acquired on their own the habit of manipulating objects. Their activities in the first test were limited; they handled a rake, a sheet, or a glass cylinder in a perfectly ordinary way without attempting to seize the fruit.

Other observers — Haggerty (30a), Shepherd (63), Kinnaman (34), and Hobhouse (31) — obtained some positive results in experiments similar to those cited above. (Each time the test involved using a rake, hook, sheet, or slip-knot to get hold of a piece of fruit; trying to remove it from a tube; pushing a swiveling rod under a hanging piece of fruit to reach it, etc.) Unfortunately, here, too, the influence of imitation is not at all clear. The animals always proceeded by trial and error. The most one can say is that example may have served to speed up the process.

Some distinctions, however, should be made. As Hobhouse has demonstrated (31), the more advanced monkeys, especially the chimpanzees, tend to solve such problems much more rapidly than the others and seem capable of imitating a greater variety of acts. The experiments conducted by Köhler (36), which are the best and the most important ever made with anthropoids, confirm this finding. But the tests always involve acts that the animal already knows or "understands." The regrouping, never instantaneous, to which Watson alludes, implies that in man there takes place a quick analytical process which breaks up the act into imitable *movements*. If my thesis is correct, this kind of pure imitation of elementary movements constitutes the most evolved, entirely human form of imitation. The monkey does not imitate meaningless gestures. Nor, contrary to popular belief, does he imitate man's facial expressions, although he may be able to respond to human provocation with spontaneous simian affective expressions. Aristotle said that of all the animals, man is the most imitative. This statement has been criticized on the ground that it applies more to monkeys than it does to man. But this ancient philosopher proved to be the better observer. His conception of genuine imitation is more accurate than that of his critics.

CONCLUSION

Summary. In examining the phenomenon of imitation, I have dealt with a significant *mental function* whose importance scarcely needs to be underscored. Through imitation, the social environment exerts an influence on the intellectual development of the child that equals that of the physical environment. This being so, it is just as impossible to explain the genesis of the mind without reference to social realities as it is to account for the development of the individual without reference to his physical experiences. Through imitation the child assimilates most of the higher, differentiated forms of activity, especially the most differentiated of all activities and their universal substitute, language.

But awareness of the influence of society on the formation of the individual conscience does not obviate the need to explain the mechanism of this influence in terms of general laws whose extension may infinitely transcend the domain of human psychology. This is precisely what I have attempted to do in investigating the means by which the very young child *learns* to imitate.

To begin with, this study has shown that example and, in a more general way, the mental image of the act, do not from the very outset possess a special efficiency; rather, this efficiency is acquired by first stimulating, then controlling the "attempts" to achieve imitation.

After examining the mechanism more closely, I found that the impact of example was in most instances much more indirect than I had assumed. And, to be sure, since the act of the model and that of the child are usually perceived very differently, the function of example as a control generally operates only in regard to the external aspect or objective effects of the act. Yet it is these acts that determine to a large extent the movements themselves. For this the inherited system of sensory-motor reactions is responsible. To such a formative cause convergent influences are added. First comes the influence of an experience that transforms instincts into more precise habitual adaptations. This acts on the child in precisely the same way it acts on the man. Finally comes the influence of education, in the narrow sense of the word — that is, the kind of training that can hardly be called artificial and that intervenes in most children to accelerate the normal evolution of habits. But, in the course of this adaptation, the law of transference tends more and more to subordinate perception of the model's movements to acts which at first were dependent upon special objects or cues.

Genuine imitation begins the moment that interdependence of common perceptible effects lends a suggestive quality, a motor and affective significance, to the gestures of others. Imitation can thus become constructive, creative. It can fulfill its social function not only by generalizing the individual reactions comprised within the framework of already familiar acts (that is, by producing coordinated movements) but also by enabling the individual to adapt himself to ways of behaving that are new to him. This holds true whether such new ways are the consequence of collective tradition or the result of truly individual initiatives.

It was also on the basis of the law of transference that I ventured to explain awareness of imitation and progress in imitation. Assimilation evolves from without to within, from objective effects to the movements that produce them. It seems to me that awareness of imitation is inseparable from the development of the notion of self in the child. Imitation enables the child to see himself in the person of another. This objective image is the nucleus within which affective personal impressions are condensed — impressions that are in themselves incapable of becoming distinct objects of thought.

Finally, I have described the affective aspects of assimilation: sympathy, envy, jealousy. These feelings, whose emergence has already been traced, tend increasingly to typify progress in imitation, to the detriment of other sentiments that are often quite different.

The Problem of Instinct. Even if the validity of the foregoing conclusions is acceptable, it will still be necessary, in order to make my point of view completely plausible, to elaborate on one point.

This has to do with a highly significant problem in psychology, one that requires a new and separate study.

It would be incorrect to say that I have described imitation as being dependent on accidental associations. The transferences examined in the preceding pages are based on the existence of the family and society, as well as on the underlying factors that subordinate the child to the man. But does the role of associations completely exclude the idea of an instinctive preformation? Does the term *instinctive imitation* have no meaning at all?

I have sought to circumscribe the role of instincts by demonstrating their importance in the sensory-motor reactions that dominate the domain of relationships in general, the relations of the organism to the physical environment. But I reject the notion that perception of the human person and his acts can determine instinctive imitation. This does not mean that imitation owes nothing to instinct. Actually, the very opposite is true.

If, as James claims, man possesses more instincts than other creatures, it is likewise true that it is the most difficult thing in the world to prove that pure instinct exists in man. No act exists that does not have instinctual roots. On the other hand, no act can be explained solely in terms of these instinctual roots. My own observations point to the existence of instincts which experience and tradition make more precise; they also point to acts whose aspects have already been modified by associative phenomena. Consequently, it seems to me that the nature of these acts can be defined only as a residuum of analytical observation.

The idea of an instinctual tendency is legitimate whenever a definite excitomotor reaction is involved — in other words, when an exact indication is given of the stimuli that elicit such a reaction and of the objective consequences that produce it. The preformation of an instinctual tendency is therefore that of the nervous system to which it corresponds. The power of an instinctual tendency resides in the very excitability of this system, whose sensitivity might well vary under the impact of diverse influences (such as those, for example, that presuppose the play of humoral theories). But this notion lacks precision, as is evident from even a casual observation of the *general nature* of reactions and stimuli. Not only is there a tendency to make concrete an abstraction, a hidden cause that fails to provide a true explanation; the meaning of the term as a mere designation for a category of facts is entirely ambiguous. To speak of the instinct of self-preservation, or the imitative instinct, is to employ a very vague expression. In no way does it tell us *which acts* this instinct inspires in the individual, or *under what conditions* he executes them. It does not distinguish them from many other acts which may fit into this conceptual framework just as easily, but which are not real. Finally, the very indeterminate character of the notion leaves unchallenged the assumption that purely instinctual reactions, which tend to be confused with the totality of acts stemming from them, are influenced by association, custom, and reflection.

It is conceivable that the best way of resolving the question is to give up the quest for an abstract definition and return to a more experimental determination of the primordial sensory-motor reactions. Once such primitive data are better understood, it may be possible to follow their ultimate evolution and show how complicated they become under the influence of associative phenomena. This is the method I have attempted to apply, while remaining ever mindful of how incomplete present-day analysis of primitive data continues to be.

If one child is more envious than another, this cannot be explained by the more powerful attraction exerted on him by the desired object. What makes the object so desirable to him is the fact of having seen it in the hands of *someone else*. Similarly, in the choice of the model, the seduction is excited not only by the act in question but also by the prestige of the agent. I am therefore tempted to conclude that what is involved here is a tendency that is innate, an already definite *predisposition* that had been waiting — in some sort of guise about which I know nothing — for a subsequent experience, that of man and social relations, to take place and to endow it with genuine content. But, as I have indicated elsewhere, this is not very satisfying. More research will have to be done. It will be necessary to penetrate beyond the tendencies of people or situations in which they play a part until we arrive at the primitive reactions implicit in the relations of the child with people. This is difficult to analyze because of the extreme complexity of such a conception of man, around whom affective life becomes polarized. A very large number of primitive reactions therefore become involved each time that affective life is stimulated. This explains individual differences in energy and in the quality of derived tendencies.

To push this analysis further — I have merely touched upon it here — the researcher will probably have to broaden his approach. The monographic method of pursuing subjects step by step in their mental development may be appropriate in studying an individual record of imitation and the mechanism of the imitative process. But, on the other hand, the comparative method may well be employed in order to fix the various elementary, primitive tendencies that compose a good part of the data on imitation and that determine its orientation and scope. Such a method will have to lean heavily on data regarding pathology and animal psychology as well as on the results of sociological investigations.

WORKS CITED

1. Baldwin, J. M. 1895. *Mental development in the child and the race: Methods and processes.* New York: Macmillan Co.
2. ———. 1899. *Social and ethical interpretations in mental development: A study in social psychology.* New York: Macmillan Co.
3. Berry. 1908. An experimental study of imitation in cats. *J. Comp. Neur. Psych.*
4. ———. 1906. The imitative tendencies of the white rat. *J. Comp. Neur. Psych.*
5. Binet. 1909. Peut-on enseigner la parole aux sourds-muets? *Année psych.*
6. Bloch. 1921. Les premiers stades du langage de l'enfant. *J. psych.*
7. Boutan. 1913. *Psuedo-langage.* Bordeaux (from de Reul, P. Bulletin de l'Institut Solvay, 1914).
8. Breed. 1911. The development of certain instincts and habits in chicks. *Behavior Monographs* 1.
9. Buhler. 1922. *Die geistige Entwicklung des Kindes.* Jena: Fisher.
10. Claparède. 1916. *Psychologie de l'enfant.* Geneva: Kindig.

NOTE: Numbers 3, 4, 7, 8, 12, 30*a*, and 60 could not be consulted in the original.

11. Cole. 1919. The senses and instincts of the raccoon. *J. Animal Behavior.*
12. ———. 1907. Concerning the intelligence of raccons. *J. Comp. Neur. Psych.*
13. Collin, A. 1914. *Le développement de l'enfant.* Paris: Doin.
14. Compayré. 1896. *Le développement mental de l'enfant.* Paris: Alcan.
15. Conradi. 1905. Song and call notes of English sparrows when reared by canaries. *Amer. J. Psych.*
16. Craig. 1912. Observations on doves learning to drink. *J. Animal Behavior.*
17. ———. 1914. Male doves reared in isolation. *J. Animal Behavior.*
18. Cramaussel. 1911. *Le premier éveil de l'intelligence.* Paris: Alcan.

19. Darwin. 1873. *The expression of the emotions in man and animals.* New York: D. Appleton.
20. Delacroix. 1921. De l'automatisme dans l'imitation. *J. Psych.*
21. ———. 1924. *Le langage et la pensée.* Paris: Alcan.
22. Dumas. 1920. L'interpsychologie. *J. Psych.*
23. ———. 1922. *Traité de psychologie.* Vol. 1, chap. 1. Paris: Alcan.
24. Ferretti. 1919. L'Imitazione e l'Infancia. *Rivista de Psicologia.*
25. Finnbogason. 1914. *L'intelligence sympathique.* Paris: Alcan.
26. Groos. 1902. *Les jeux des animaux.* Paris: Alcan.
27. ———. 1921. *Das Seelenleben des Kindes.* 5th ed. Berlin: Reuther and Richard.
28. Gutzmann. 1894. *Sprache und Sprachfehler.* Leipzig: Weber.
29. ———. 1924. *Handbuch der vergleichenden Psychologie.* From Kafka, vol. 2 (Psych. der Sprache). Munich: Reinhardt.
30. ———. 1913. Ueber Gewohnung und Gewohnheit. *Fortschritte der Psychologie.*
30a. Haggerty. 1909. Imitation in monkeys. *J. Comp. Neur. Psych.*
30b. Hachet-Souplet. 1913. *De l'animal à l'enfant.* Paris: Alcan.
31. Hobhouse. 1911. *Mind in evolution.* London: Macmillan.
32. Holmes. 1911. *The Evolution of animal intelligence.* New York: Holt.
33. Kafka. 1923. *Handbuch der vergleichenden Psychologie*: 1. *Tierpsychologie.* Munich: Reinhardt.
34. Kinnaman. 1902. Mental life of two macacus rhesus monkeys in captivity. *Amer. J. Psych.*
35. Koffka. 1921. *Die Grundlagen der psychischen Entwicklung.* Oesterwieck: Ziegfeldt.
36. Köhler. 1917. *Intelligenz prufungen an Anthropoïden.* Abhandlungen der Königl. Berlin: Akademie des Wissenschaften.
37. Köhler. 1921. Zur Psychologie der Schimpansen. *Psych. Forschung* 1:1–2.
38. Lashley. 1913. Reproduction of inarticulate sounds in the parrot. *J. Animal Behavior.*
39. Le Dantec. 1899. Le mécanisme de l'imitation. *Rev. phil.*
40. Leroy, B. 1905. *Le langage.* Paris: Alcan.
41. Lipps. 1909. *Leitfaden der Psychologie.* Leipzig: Engelmann.
42. Luquet. 1913. *Les dessins d'un enfant.* Paris: Alcan.
43. MacDougall. 1923. *An introduction to social psychology.* 18th ed.
44. Magnat. 1874. *Cours d'articulation.* Paris: Sandoz.
45. Marichelle. 1910. *L'enseignement de la parole aux sourd-smuets.* Grenoble: Allier.
46. Marie, P. 1922. *Existe-t-il des centres innés pour le langage?* Questions neurologiques actuelles. Paris: Masson.

46a. Morgan, C. L. 1896. *Habit and instinct*. London: Arnold.
47. Paulhan, J. 1907. L'imitation dans l'idée du moi. *Rev. phil.*
48. Pawlowitch. 1920. *Le langage enfantin*. Paris: Champion.
49. Perez, B. 1902. *Les trois premières années de l'enfant*. 6th ed. Paris: Alcan.
50. Piaget. 1923. *Le langage et la pensée chez l'enfant*. Neuchâtel and Paris: Delachaux and Niestlé.
51. Pioger. 1900. *La surdi-mutité: Procédés d'enseignement*. Asnières.
52. Porter. 1910. Intelligence and imitation in birds. *Amer. J. Psych.*
53. Prandlt. 1910. *Die Einfühlung*. Leipzig: Barth.
54. Preyer. 1887. *L'âme de l'enfant*. Paris: Alcan.
55. Queyrat. 1905. *Les jeux des enfants*. Paris: Alcan.
56. Ribot. 1914. *La psychologie des sentiments*. 9th ed. Paris: Alcan.
57. Ronijat. 1913. *Le développement du langage chez un enfant bilingue*.
58. Schaefer. 1913. *Beitraege zur Kinderforschung*. Paris: Alcan.
59. Schjelderup-Ebbe. 1922, 1923. Beitraege zur social und individuel psychologie des Haushuns. *Zietschrift für Psychologie*.
60. Scott. 1901. Song in birds. *Science*.
60a. ———. 1902. Data on song in birds. *Science*.
60b. ———. 1904. The inheritance of songs. *Science*.
61. Scupin. 1907. *Bubis erste Kindheit*. Leipzig: Griebens.
62. Shepherd. 1911. Imitation in raccoons. *Amer. J. Psych.*
63. ———. 1910. Some mental processes of the rhesus monkeys. *Psych. Monographs*.
64. Shinn. 1893–99. *Notes on the development of a child*. Berkeley.
65. Small. 1900. An experimental study of the mental processes of the rat. *Amer. J. Psych.*
66. Smith. 1915. *Mind in animals*. Cambridge: Univ. Press.
67. Spencer, H. 1892. *Principes de psychologie*. 2: *Sociabilité et sympathie*. Paris: Alcan.
68. Stern, W. 1907. *Die Kindersprache*. Leipzig: Barth.
69. ———. 1921. *Psychologie der frühen Kindheit*. 2d ed. Leipzig: Quelle and Meyer.
70. Sully. 1898. *Etudes sur l'enfance*. Paris: Alcan.
71. Taine. 1876. Observations sur l'acquisition du langage par les enfants. *Rev. phil.*
72. Thorndike, 1911. *Animal intelligence*. New York: Macmillan.
73. ———. 1913. *The original nature of man*. New York: Columbia University.
74. Vigouroux and Juquelier. 1904. *La contagion mentale*. Paris: Doin.
75. Villey, P. 1918. *Le monde des aveugles*. Paris: Flammarion.

76. ———. 1922. *La pédagogie des aveugles*. Paris: Alcan.
77. Watson. 1914. *Behavior: An introduction to comparative psychology*. New York: Holt.
78. ———. 1908. Imitation in monkeys. *Psych. Bulletin*.
79. Woodworth. 1899. *The accuracy of voluntary movement*. New York: Macmillan Co.
80. Yerkes. 1916. The mental life of monkeys and apes. *Behavior Monographs* 3.